Almost Green

Almost Green

*How I Saved $\frac{1}{6}$th of a Billionth
of the Planet*

James Glave

SKYHORSE PUBLISHING

Skyhorse Publishing books may be purchased in bulk at special discounts for
sales promotion, corporate gifts, fund raising, or educational purposes. Special
editions can also be created to specifications. For details, contact the Special
Sales Department, Skyhorse Publishing, 555 Eighth Avenue, Suite 903, New
York, NY 10018 or info@skyhorsepublishing.com.

www.skyhorsepublishing.com

10 9 8 7 6 5 4 3 2 1

Library of Congress Cataloging-in-Publication Data

Glave, James.
Almost green : how I saved 1/6th of a billionth of the planet / James
Glave.
p. cm.
ISBN 978-1-60239-286-1 (alk. paper)
1. Environmental protection--Humor. 2. Suburban life--Humor.
I. Title.
PN6231.E66G53 2008
690'.8047092--dc22
2008013180
Printed in the United States of America

For Sabrina and Duncan.

May we not let you down.

Contents

Prologue

My name is James, and I drive an SUV. It is a golden-pearl premium edition Lexus RX 300, with all-leather interior, genuine walnut wood dash, seven-speaker Nakamichi sound system, seat heaters, moon-roof, and sport racks. It is a high-riding icon of luxury, a mobile conspicuous-consumption statement, a prosperity public-address system—the sort of vehicle that valets named Chip park in front of five-star Indian-fusion restaurants. Let me be clear, though, that the RX 300 is not an indication of my hard-won success as a writer. It's a hand-me-down from my father-in-law, who offered it to my wife, Elle, and me as a gift just as our 1994 Volvo station wagon threatened to die with our two tired babies in the back-seat some night on a lonely New Mexico byway well beyond the fringes of Verizon's digital safety net. Although we are extremely grateful for the gift, the Lexus was perhaps not our first choice for a family four-door vehicle; it conveys a not-entirely-accurate message about who we are to those who don't know us.

This became clear to me one day when I had lunch with my friend Dave, a former colleague whom I greatly admire. It had been a few years since we'd seen each other, and we were sharing a laugh over a certain local restaurant critic who we both felt could benefit from a little more journalistic backbone. Dave was describing his most recent sighting of the foodie scribe in question: "I'm sitting in this sidewalk café, right? And up pulls you-know-who in this total *asshole Lexus SUV.*"

Hilarious. For at least a few months after that day—at least when out of earshot of our small children—Elle and I referred to our golden-pearl palace on wheels as "the asshole."

And please forgive me, Padre. Because even though you have that framed photo of George Bush, Sr., in your office, and even though you forward me e-mails asserting that global warming is a "swindle" and a "liberal conspiracy," I do really love you, and I so appreciate your generosity. But the more I read up on the damage I am doing each time I motor through another tank of regular unleaded, the more I can relate to Dave's point of view and the less comfortable I am getting back behind the wheel. Because I am the one running a scam.

We have hung on to your wheels for reasons that contradict our gradually increasing consciousness and have everything to do with cash flow and guilt. We don't want to offend you, and we don't want to finance something else. I don't think we can keep dancing like this forever, though. One day I'm going to have to break it to you, Padre, that I think your very generous six-cylinder endowment is gradually torching the lot of us.

For now, assuming Pops doesn't care either way, Elle and I are looking to downsize. With the kids now out of strollers and diapers, we've finally decommissioned our bulky toddler infrastructure. We are in the market for a small car. I've brought my preschool-age son Duncan and his five-year-old sister, Sabrina, into the loop, and they have already begun window-shopping with me as we tool around the twenty-five-square-mile island we call home, just off the sparkling West Coast city of Vancouver, B.C., Canada. One recent morning, on the way to day care, my son asked me to explain the differences between our all-wheel-drive beast and the zippy little DaimlerChrysler Smart Car that had just passed us headed the other direction.

"Dad," he asked, "why don't we have a Smart Car?"

Let me briefly mention here that, like many young boys, my Duncan is infatuated with internal combustion. If it drives, digs, or flies via some flavor of refined petroleum, well, he's got its number.

"They're fun, aren't they?" I replied. "We don't have one because they're too small. There isn't enough room inside one of them for our whole family."

"Why not?" Sabrina chimed in.

"Well, there are four people in our family, and the Smart Car only fits two people. So we would have to take turns or sit on each other's lap, and that wouldn't work very well, would it?"

"Oh. OK."

I could have left it there, but I didn't. "It *is* possible to have a car that's too big, though. Mummy and Daddy think this car is too big. That's why we are hoping to trade it for a smaller one."

"Why do we want a smaller one?" asked Sabrina.

"Well, honey, you know how we always stop at the gas station to buy gasoline? This car is pretty heavy—it's much heavier than it needs to be—and so it uses up more gas than a Smart Car. Gas is expensive, and it is also very bad for the Earth."

"But Dad," said Duncan, "why is gas bad for the Earth?"

Long pause here. *Jesus, where do I begin?*

"Hmmm. OK, when we burn gas it makes the car go, but it also makes the Earth get hotter. And we're worried that if we burn too much gas, the Earth will get too hot, and it won't be such a nice place to live when you two grow up."

"So our car is too heavy for the Earth?"

"Yes, that's right. We want to get a smaller car that all four of us can fit inside, one that uses less gas—one that's nicer to the planet."

"But not a Smart Car?" confirmed Duncan.

"Right. Not a Smart Car. There are lots of other kinds of smaller cars out there."

"What kind of car do you want?" Sabrina queried.

"Well, Mummy and Daddy would really like to get a car called a Prius," I said, offering to point out the next one we passed.

"A Prius? Why do we want that one?"

"Because it doesn't use as much gas, so it's nicer to the planet. And we can all fit inside one."

"Why don't we get one of those cars right now?"

"Um, they are expensive. They cost too much money for us, sweets. But we'll figure it out. In the meantime, we are trying to use this car less. That's why we walk to the village together so much."

"Oh," replied Sabrina. "Oh, yeah."

I grinned to myself. Duncan was hopelessly obsessed with fuel injectors and five-speed manual transmissions, but his older sister had just made the right connections in her head. She's a smart cookie, this girl of mine. I was proud of her, and proud of myself for explaining that our present vehicle wasn't so great but that answers were out there. I'd slipped in an age-appropriate explanation of climate change, without coloring in the whole grim picture.

Then Sabrina chimed in again with a pearl of wisdom that put all my eco-angst into perspective the way only a precocious five-year-old can.

"You know what, Dad?"

"Hmmm?"

"I have a vagina."

"Yes ...?"

"But Duncan has a Prius!"

* * *

This is a book about the construction of a sustainably designed 280-square-foot writing studio—the building I have come to call my Eco-Shed. But it is also about the making of an evolution. It is about my own ecological awakening and my personal struggle to reconcile an increasing awareness of a sick planet with a sprawling economic and political framework more or less engineered to preserve the status quo. It is about the end of the world as we know it and the promise of a better one to replace it just in time. It is about the small trade-offs we make in our heads every day between convenience and cost, entitlement and personal responsibility. It is about our natural instinct to flatten the protruding nail of personal sacrifice with the always-handy hammers of convenience and denial. It is about genuinely wanting to leave a lighter footprint on the planet but running smack up against a series of obstacles—some practical and objective, others less so—and muddling through with as much humor and grace as possible.

This book is also about a transformation that has unexpectedly unspooled between my own two ears over the course of the past year or so. Like me, you probably already know that global warming presents the single greatest threat to humanity in all of history and the most profound challenge we face as a civilization. You probably also understand that the Big Melt is not just another "environmental problem" we need to worry about. Instead, it has emerged as the defining moral, ethical, and economic issue of our time.

But like me, you also live in the real world. A world in which you still have to get to work by 8:30. One in which the kids need to be at swimming lessons on Saturday. One in which your benevolent father-in-law gives you a late-model import SUV for Christmas, then builds you a seventeen-thousand-dollar timber-framed double carport to park it in.

Transformational change is a messy, sometimes awkward business. As in Sabrina's ultra-mega-blockbuster crayon collection, there are multiple shades of green. There's what I like to call "baseline" green, the color of normalized everyday activities and behaviors—curbside recycling, backyard composting, and USDA Certified Organic whatever. But travel a little further along the continuum—move beyond these everyday norms and dabble with a slightly darker shade of green—and things start to get complicated. By way of example, it's all well and good to say "Enough, already, with all the air travel" but not so easy if your wife's family and lifelong friends are scattered widely across the continent. It doesn't take long to figure out why those who work the hardest to make the world a better place can easily find themselves not fitting into it very well. In this carbon-counting age, a thin line separates the leaders from the sanctimonious jerks.

How does one embrace a greener life and keep everybody in it happy along the way? How do we gently redirect our dear Duncan, who equates petroleum with power and control and liberty and adventure—feelings he is hardwired to covet—without turning him into a playground weirdo? How do I inspire my friends, family, and neighbors without making them feel either inadequate or defensive? And more to the point, how do we get rid of our damn SUV without throwing a metaphorical family piston rod, casting shards of broken steel through the engine compartment of our reasonably well-running marriage? And speaking of marriage, how do I convince my wife to turn off the damn energy-sucking halogen lights that she insists on leaving on over the kitchen stove? How, in other words, do we transform our lives without unraveling them?

We live in a tortured age—rife with elaborate guilt trips, look-the-other-way hypocrisy, newfangled codes of ecological conduct, and everyday paradoxes. I am at times my own worst enemy. In summertime, I buy or pick organic, locally grown berries, then gleefully slather them with Cool Whip—likely one of the most processed foods available, if you could even call it a food. Every other week, I load boxes of tin cans, newspapers, and carefully rinsed plastic milk jugs into my SUV and drive them to the recycling depot, an exercise in ecological self-cancellation. Some of my behavior runs roughshod over my intentions, and I muddle forward, doing the best I can.

* * *

It was easier in the good old days. For years, I flipped past news stories and magazine articles about the latest atmospheric red flag: hurricanes, fires, cracking ice shelves, gaunt polar bears, and so on. With so much out there already fighting for my attention—work, family, and those precious few diversions from work and family—I knew just enough about global warming to know that everything about it was hopeless and bleak and insurmountable.

Part of the problem was that I resented the solution. It meant I needed to either inconvenience myself or descend further into consumer debt. Either drive less, the greener-thans said, or buy a more efficient car I couldn't afford. But with a mortgage and two babies, I was already living close to the edge of both my pay stub and my strategic reserves of life force. Yet the advice was the same: Turn down the thermostat another degree or two and wear a thicker sweater, or retire that old wheezing furnace altogether and invest in a new one. Choose local and organic food, which is tastier and burns less petroleum on its journey to my plate but is twice the price of the bulk packs stacked up at the Big Box store. It's human nature to take the path of least resistance, and in many cases, that's precisely what this bleary-eyed, working-stiff dad did.

Meanwhile, the greener-thans tried seducing me with baby steps. Some even packaged the changes up as eco-hedonism, underscoring the simple pleasures of a greener life. As a compulsive recycler, enthusiastic composter, and frequent cyclist, I was already—to crib the language of social marketers—"predisposed." But somewhere along the path to enlightenment, I hit a wall. I'd already swapped out my lightbulbs with more expensive models that promised to slash my monthly utility bill by 18.4 cents. But that was as far as I could go. I wasn't prepared to tack a

$386 Toyota Prius payment onto my strained monthly budget. I'd rather pump that money into the bottomless tank of my suv, the one with more room for the stroller and the groceries.

Why? To answer that, we need to rewind a little further. As a journalist, I am by trade something of a professional skeptic. My career has always been about hunches and the inner voice of curiosity, and I have always tempered "the next big thing" with the cold water of reality. At some point in late 2005, that curiosity led me to do some digging into the sustainability movement, which, by that point, had largely edged classic save-the-owls environmentalism off the radar. Having spent years out on the margins, the greens had crept back onto the pop culture agenda by refashioning themselves as champions of eco-chic. Suddenly, environmentalism wasn't about camping out in a tree and eating carob bars or buzzing Japanese whalers in Zodiacs. The new eco-movement was sexy and stylish, all gorgeous bamboo paneling and sleek wafer-thin photovoltaic panels. It wasn't about grave problems anymore; it was about easy solutions. Every other new municipal building going up was certified "green," while Hollywood starlets were giving once-dorky hybrids much-needed va-va-vroom. Hey, Cameron Diaz drives one, and she's pretty hot, right?

I wanted to peel back eco-chic's veneer and get at the meaty stuff I suspected lay underneath. I wanted to reverse-engineer the trend. To be honest, a part of me secretly wanted to take it down a notch or two.

You see, to this jaded skeptic, eco-chic wasn't about changing the world; it was about changing your furniture. You, too, can be green just like George Clooney, Brad Pitt, and Julia Roberts, the new movement promised. Just shun all that nasty plastic—except, that is, the kind in your wallet. Stick a polyurethane-free, latex-stuffed sofa bed over here ($4,500), some recycled-glass mosaic tile accents there ($55 a square foot), park a designer Dutch city bicycle ($1,500) in the front hall, and on and on. Though in principle these things were all of course far kinder to Mother Gaia—polyurethane sofa cushions are damn nasty, and not even Padre would dare dis a bicycle—none of them really required any serious reconsideration of our produce-consume-dispose economic treadmill. If eco-chic had a subtle motto, it was this: "Shop different, feel better." Though I admittedly wasn't making much of a difference myself, I knew, somewhere deep down, we all needed to do more. Much more.

Then a funny thing happened on the way to the Toyota dealership: in the name of due diligence, I drank the Kool-Aid. The more I educated myself about what was going on in the blue skies overhead, the more I realized that revisiting my own habits, at the checkout counter, around the house, and in the car, wasn't just the right thing to do—it was a moral imperative. I gradually came to realize that climate change wasn't some abstract, bummer, out-there issue fighting for my attention like, say, my neglected retirement savings or a long-planned videotaped home inventory. No, it was about my two preschool-age children and the children they might have someday. Not to get all terribly earnest, but it stirred inside me the same sort of compulsion to do something that I imagine my British grandparents must have felt as they watched Hitler and his thugs march across Western Europe.

I resolved to change the things I could and try not to worry too much about the things I couldn't. Although I was hopelessly jealous of the swish Ford Escape Hybrid that a physician friend had bought for his family, my wife and I had already sold one of our two carbon-spewing suvs, so we tried to feel good about that. Problem is, I soon ended up where I am today, at the start of a year of green renewal, in a kind of eco-neurotic feedback loop. I am by nature a chronic worrywart. It's my mother's fault, really (sorry, Mum). From her, I inherited a nasty nail-biting habit and a low-level-anxiety gene, which I have incidentally passed along to my girl Sabrina, the poor thing. It's more a background anxiousness than a clinical anxiety, nothing that would warrant a regimen of pharmaceuticals—at least not yet. But thanks to my mild personality quirk, I can no longer hide from what I now understand. My newfound ecological literacy suffuses even the mundane routines of my daily life. Some days, inside my head, the end of the world just won't go away.

So, welcome to my one-man recyclables-sorting sideshow, set against a backdrop of creeping collective dread. Pour yourself a drink, throw in some ice—hey, the grid is still up; the freezer's full of it, right?—and enjoy the ride.

Creation

I n December 2005, before Arnie became a real-life action
hero, before Wal-Mart tried on a green suit, before the age
of the carbon-neutral wedding, before Al Gore snagged
half of a Nobel Peace Prize—before, in other words, the tipping
point began to tip—a clever batch of British bureaucrats released
a two-minute celluloid gem to the world.

With Katrina still very much a household name, a UK government agency called the Department for Environment, Food,
and Rural Affairs released a film called *Tomorrow's Climate,
Today's Challenge* to Britain's television programming directors,
who slotted it in on prime time alongside the ads for Cadbury's
chocolate and Persil washing powder. It has since aired in front
of millions of Britons.

The clip—catch it on YouTube—opens with a spinning planet
Earth seen from space, then zooms in as a narrator quickly sum-
marizes the science of global warming before getting to the good
part. The trouble with carbon dioxide, he notes, is that the stuff
is invisible. "If we could see the gases," he explains, "the problem

would be obvious to everyone." And so, in a chilling montage sequence, digital-effects gurus do the job for us—decorating a series of tractors, passenger jets, cars, and factories with menacing upward-spiraling purple plumes. The technique is simple, its impact devastating; the sequence sends your heart plunging into your vegan-compliant shoes.

One cut leaps off my computer screen each time I obsessively trigger my mouse button to watch it. For a brief moment, an otherwise innocent line of English row houses appears on the screen spewing those purple vapors—the film's digitally rendered greenhouse gas emissions—like a Louisiana vinyl plant. It's a throat-grabbing moment, and in my mind it underscores one of the most inconvenient truths of all: increasing numbers of us connect the dots between suv tailpipes and the hottest summers on record, but we often overlook a big bad factory right under our noses—home.

The fact is, our footprint does not end at the driveway, and to prove it, I must trot out a necessarily grim statistic. A few pages earlier, I invited you to pour yourself a drink. Please set this book down for a moment, take a big swig from your glass, and let's get it out of the way: According to the Department of Energy, in 2005, residential carbon-dioxide emissions across the United States amounted to 1.3 *billion* metric tons—21 percent of the nation's overall atmospheric invoice that year. It's a big number, and it's just over 300 million metric tons bigger than it was in 1990.(Aren't you glad you're getting sloshed?)

Why the ridiculous increase? It's more people buying bigger televisions, sure, but it's also more and much larger houses heated with gigajoules of natural gas and cooled with gigawatts of coal-fired electricity. The latter "dirty" energy brews the morning coffee in roughly half of U.S. homes and about 17 percent of those up here in Canada, which is blessed with an abundance of mostly clean-and-green, large-scale hydroelectric generating projects. In fact, up here in the Great Wet North, household electricity is commonly referred to as simply "hydro."

But then there's the potential upside: A recent United Nations report concluded that we could head off the annual release of 45 million tons of CO_2 worldwide by 2010 simply by beefing up construction codes. That's roughly the same amount of heat-trapping bad news kicked up by thirteen medium-sized, five-hundred-megawatt coal power plants running day and night for an entire year.

But even though climate change has at last entered the realm of casual dinner conversation, even though the keenest of the green have moved the needle from "carbon neutral" to "carbon negative," many of us are still not prepared to change our domestic habits.

That was Elle and me in a nutshell: we knew what was going on up there, and why, but we weren't prepared to link it to our own actions, mostly because we felt that nobody else was, and doing so would mean forgoing the cool stuff that we'd been coached to covet. Let me give you an example: for years, Elle and I had planned an LCD-projection home theater system. When we were building our present house, a tract home on Bowen Island, British Columbia, we instructed the builder to run speaker wire into seven receptacle boxes around the living room, with the idea of eventually turning much of the main floor into a cinema. The

West Coast winters are long, dark, and wet, we figured, and there is not as of yet a six-screen multiplex on Bowen Island.

Each time Elle and I had new friends over for dinner, I'd proudly point out the blank covers on the speaker boxes around the ceiling. "We'll mount the projector up here, and that whole wall over there will become the screen," I'd explain, addressing the male half of our visiting couple. Then, inevitably, while our wives would roll their eyes and begin comparing notes on organic beef suppliers, Visiting Dude and I would geek out over the relative merits of LCD versus plasma and other competing home-entertainment technologies.

Ultimately, we'd end the conversation in a stalemate, each of us defending whichever chipset we'd already bought into.

Our first year on the island, we couldn't afford to buy and install the seven-speaker entertainment system, and just as it grew closer to our grasp, I began to ask myself if I really wanted the thing at all. One day I let it slip to Elle that I was having second thoughts.

"Oh please," she said. "Don't tell me we can't get a home theater system now!"

"I don't know, love," I said. "It's been in our plans forever, but I'm not sure I feel good about the idea. I'd like us to reduce our energy consumption, not increase it. I mean, do we really need to buy more electronics? The TV has a DVD player, and we watch movies on there all the time."

"But we really wanted that big remote-control roll-down screen and everything," she said. "You know, movie nights with popcorn, friends over? I *love* going to the movies, and we never get to see any since we moved to this island. I miss it. We planned this from the beginning."

"I'm not saying we can't have it, period," I said. "I just saying let's think about it and make sure both of us still feel OK with it, because I'm just not sure *I* do."

It seems strange to wring my hands over an LCD projector when so many people in this world don't even have running water, but problems are all relative. Perhaps it's my increasing sensitivity to energy use—or maybe it comes from living on an island or I'm just getting old—but I've grown jaded about gadgetry and appliances and gratuitous consumerism.

And that's how I felt when the MasterCard points catalog arrived. To thank us for regularly racking up thousands of dollars in high-interest consumer debt, every so often our credit union sends us a booklet full of loyalty incentives—typically, a selection of small household devices of dubious utility. A simple toll-free call to Sandra, a Mumbai-based operator with a perfectly coached Canadian accent, would bring just about any of it to our door within three business days—a reward for good consumer behavior. Once upon a time, I would have pored over the pages for hours, grooving to the selection of stainless-steel panini presses (23,700 points) or espresso makers (33,100 points), iPod clock radios (19,100 points), and AC-powered SUV mini-fridges (12,900 points). Now the thank-you-for-shopping book yields only mild ennui. All I see is page after page of pointless, flimsy, kilowatt-sucking crap. The knob will break off or the plastic tank will crack, and after a short life spent mostly taking up cabinet space and offering little of the promised joy, the 120-volt trinket will assume its ultimate place in the landfill.

Within the past year or two, as I've gradually realized the planetary consequences of unchecked growth, runaway consumption, and fossil fuel dependency, I've decided that Elle and I don't need more stuff in our house. We need better stuff, and far less of it. Although Madison Avenue still coaches us to believe that new products will make us happy, there is no meaningful satisfaction to be had from a seven-speaker home theater system or an iPod clock radio. I've discovered that if there is a subversive agenda in the nouveau-green movement, it lies in these questions: Can we reframe our definition of happiness? Can we feel good about ourselves without shopping or redecorating? Can we make choices that genuinely improve our quality of life? Can we imagine our homes as something other than commodities to be stocked with commodities?

In my mind, a home is the seat of the family. If it were smaller, simpler, easier to clean, and cheaper to run, we'd spend less time maintaining it or working to pay for it and more time enjoying it. We should do more than expect this level of return from our houses; we should demand it.

This craving to change, to reboot, to evolve, to do something really different and bold on the domestic front—and to get beyond the "baby step"—is what drove me to build the Eco-Shed, the high-performance, ultra-low-footprint studio that now stands in my front yard. To me, the structure—a building that is as green as I can afford—is more than just a bold architectural statement. It is a 280-square-foot call to arms. It is a public declaration of realigned priorities and, hopefully, a beacon of inspiration and education. But although the Eco-Shed is a modern West Coast island case study, the seeds of the project took root much farther away, in the high desert of the Southwest, in one of the oldest cities in America.

* * *

Elle and I bought our first house in April 2000 in Santa Fe, New Mexico. It was a fourteen-hundred-square-foot, two-bedroom faux adobe fixer-upper, and it came equipped with R-*nada* insulation in the walls and a wheezing, forced air furnace that sounded like a packed 737 on the takeoff roll. In winter, the tired heater—it was original to the house, which went up in 1959—fought a battle it could never win in an effort to keep the indoor temperature within the brackets on the thermostat labeled "comfort zone."

It was a hopeless task. If viewed on a frigid and snowy January night through one of the thermal scopes that pops up now and then on *CSI*, our casa would've lit up like a blazing beach bonfire. Except the vivid pixelated reds and golds that I imagine dancing on the screen would be the hot flashes of a planet in distress.

The house's infrastructure was on its last legs, but we preferred to ignore it. A new kitchen topped our to-do list, not an expensive new furnace that we'd only turn on for six months of the year. Not even brutally high natural gas bills would nudge us to open that utility closet door. During one particularly arctic winter when Elle was working from home, our monthly heating bill inched north of four hundred dollars—and that was with the thermostat set to fifty degrees F. I vividly remember the day she went to the mailbox and opened that particular envelope, because she called me at work.

"What the hell is this?" Elle demanded. It was as if a collection agency had just inquired about a secret credit card account that I'd maxed out with Internet porn charges.

"It's our *gas bill,* hon. It's winter, and you know as well as I do that our house is full of leaks and holes."

"We can't afford this!" she wailed.

I tried to calm her down. "Look, it's simple. We can spend four hundred dollars a month on natural gas until the spring thaw, or we can replace the furnace, order extra insulation, replace the doors, insulate the water pipes, and so on, which will cost us, oh, around thirty thousand dollars."

"We can't afford that, either!"

"Well, which do you want?"

"I'm so pissed! I'm not giving all our money to those mofos!"

Elle hung up and cranked the thermostat down to the "discomfort zone." For much of the rest of the winter, she worked in the home office dressed like a construction worker, wearing fingerless gloves, a down jacket, a scarf, a ski hat, and down booties—a petty act of consumer disobedience noticed by pretty much nobody except the startled FedEx guy. The stunt brought the bill down around a hundred dollars or so.

A retrofit would have made a difference to our Santa Fe home, but only to a degree. That's because, as in tens of millions of other midcentury American homes, the exterior walls of the place were built with two-by-four lumber. We could have drilled into the stud cavities and pumped the spaces with blow-in cellulose insulation, but thanks to a phenomenon known as thermal bridging, the home's skimpy wood skeleton would've simply wicked much of our precious warmth straight out into the cold, dry, high-desert air.

As for the doors and windows, I once tried to weatherstrip our warped front entrance but ended up throwing the whole roll of sticky-backed foam tape into the junipers. My efforts to seal those gaps and cracks proved futile—either the door wouldn't close or it ripped off the foam strips every time we opened it. We needed to replace the door entirely. But that was second in line after the paper-thin single-pane windows, which we did swap for new double-glazed vinyl panes after the first winter. They looked very nice, but still we froze.

Our abode was designed and built in an era when energy was cheap and seemingly limitless, when the greenhouse effect was something that warmed a little solarium off the living room. The median age of U.S. homes is thirty-five, and although Americans spent almost $300 billion remodeling in 2006, we can be certain much of that money went where ours did: to a gleaming new all-stainless-steel kitchen. In a recent summary of trends, the National Association of the Remodeling Industry nods to new interest in eco-chic bamboo flooring but puts bigger bank in wine fridges, bathroom television sets, and, yes, LCD and plasma home theaters. Green living may be all the rage, but putting the pocketbook behind it is another matter.

In early 2003, after a few more of those Southwest Siberian winters, we began firming up loose plans to move north to my home turf of British Columbia, where my family still lived. It was time for a career remodel for me, and with our second baby in the picture, we wanted to be closer to retired grandparents.

After realizing we couldn't afford to live in downtown Vancouver—and agreeing that we really didn't want to, for reasons we will get to momentarily—we'd set our sights on nearby Bowen Island. It offered a charming village, a good school, and enough grocery stores, restaurants, and coffee shops to take care of the 3,500-odd souls who lived there. Bowen was a genuine community, where people volunteered, left their cars unlocked, and checked in on sick friends. There was a small-town parade in the summer—complete with waving firemen and a Dog of the Year float—and Santa Claus arrived, to a rock star ovation, each Christmas via water taxi.

We knew we would be building a new home when we realized the house we wanted didn't yet exist where we wanted it—within walking distance of the dock and the ferry that would take one of us to a job that could service a mortgage. Since undeveloped land was scarce, we put down five thousand dollars to reserve our choice of a series of lots slated to be logged, blasted, and built upon—the latest phase in a family-oriented development on the hillside just above the island's village.

We knew we'd get huge energy-efficiency gains over our Santa Fe place by dint of twenty-first-century building codes, but we hoped for more. We pined for a nest that at least nodded in the direction of green-building practices.

We clipped ads for tankless hot-water heaters, looked into cork flooring, and boned up on rainwater harvesting. We calculated our equity, guesstimated our earning power, ran endless scenarios, and, in the end, brought the whole package—wrapped up with a fat rubber band—to a boutique Vancouver architecture firm. That bulging file folder represented the pinnacle of our eco-modern dream, the point at which our yearning for a smaller ecological footprint clashed with our hunger for guilty pleasures—not to mention our decidedly middle-class income.

We had two choices. We could either purchase one of the new lots outright and contract with our own architect and builder, or buy one from the developer and simultaneously enter into a contract with him to build our choice of a short list of spec designs, each of which included a generous variety of upgrades and options, some green-minded, some less so. Although a little too Arts-and-Craftsy for our tastes, the houses built in the development's earlier phases seemed solid, reasonably well sited, and generally well designed.

All of the twenty available parcels offered ocean and mountain vistas, though two offered primo sightlines. One was an inexpensive 0.2-acre lot that would have a house flanking either side; the other was a loftier perch, with more privacy and epic views on almost an acre of greenbelt. Had we chosen Door No. 1—the smaller and considerably cheaper site—we might have had enough cash left over to pursue the custom eco-home. The land behind Door No. 2, however, would have gutted the budget, leaving barely enough coin for an out-of-the-box house.

The architects we met with were really nice people. They quoted us $150 per square foot, plus $26,000 or so in fees. Owing to our ill-advised career choices, the numbers refused to add up, even for what they described as a "minimally finished" and/or "phased" (read: partially built) home—let alone one equipped with, say, a planted roof. But as we struggled to make the right choice—we still lived several thousand miles away, and our two babies were keeping us exhausted and near brain-dead—it came down to a question of space. And how much of it we would need. Because if we could squeeze into a smaller house, we might be able to afford a greener one.

"There's no way we'll be happy in anything less than two thousand square feet," I declared to Elle in one of the many heated evenings that we spent—our babies finally down for the night—hashing out our real-estate conundrums.

"No. We just don't we need that much," my wife stubbornly insisted. She had an edge on the argument; she'd just read Sarah Susanka's *The Not So Big House* and had spent five years living in Germany, the spiritual home of green thinking, building, and living.

"In Europe, it was much more about smaller homes, with very efficient layouts," she said. "I mean, look at *this* house; it's almost fifteen hundred square feet, and we don't even use *half* of the living room. It's such a poor layout that much of it is wasted space. I bet we could do fine with this much space. Maybe even less."

I disagreed. "Look, we have two kids, and they're only going to get bigger. They're gonna need space to store all their soccer balls and hockey gear—all that crap. There's no way we can do it with less than two thousand."

Elle dug in her heels. "It's not how much footage you have that matters, it's how you design it! If we hire an architect to plan the space so that we actually *use* every bit of it, we won't have to buy as much house."

"Yeah, but an architect means custom building, and it doesn't look as though we can afford that. We have to go with the spec designs. And there's only one on the list with three bedrooms that's less than twenty-two hundred square feet—which will cost too much—and it's eighteen hundred square feet."

We went around and around like this for days. If home buying is an emotional roller coaster, home *building* is an emotional space shuttle launch during a Florida hurricane. It dredges up the really gory stuff that is the total of our sense of self: entitlement, need, respect, worth, sacrifice, risk, gratification. Our nerves were raw from too many late-night deadlines and toddler tantrums. Our hearts were both in the right place. But in the end, we felt too vulnerable to go for the green gusto.

We're still not sure we made the right decision. But we wrote the architects a Dear John letter and settled on an eighteen-hundred-square-foot spec home on the bigger, more private parcel of land at the end of the cul-de-sac, at the top of the hill, nestled up against a forest of cedar, hemlock, fir, and maple. We could learn to love the bungalow detailing of the spec homes. Perhaps, we postulated, the developer would be open to some changes?

He was—at first. Spec builders make their money by quoting a fixed price for a home and building their overhead and profit into the figure. They use familiar materials from reliable suppliers and run a tight, well-tuned schedule. Less back-and-forth, less hassle, and less paperwork keep the price down.

Those buying into such projects typically choose cabinet doors and countertops, maybe carpet or tile. But this developer was generous, offering pages of options for upgrades, swap-outs, and deletions. The company officially encouraged us to tweak things to our liking, within reason.

And so we did. Out went the granite-faced propane fireplace, which we wanted to replace with a swish, airtight Rais wood-stove from Denmark. The ultra-efficient $7,500 carbon-neutral stove would not only look cool but also reduce our dependence on the electric baseboard heaters. Plus, we reckoned, after about thirty-five years of use, it would pay for itself.

We also signed on for a twelve-hundred-gallon rainwater-harvesting system, a listed $4,500 out-of-pocket upgrade option, for more responsible landscaping. We dumped an extra four grand into the appliance budget and specified ultraefficient models; thanks to precision German engineering, our Miele dishwasher uses as little as 1.3 gallons of water per load. Negotiations went on from there. Bamboo flooring? No can do. Clear-cut Douglas fir it was. Skylight in the master bedroom? Check. Tankless hot-water heater? Naw, too buggy. And on it went.

Eventually, as the change orders piled up—in the end, totaling $34,300—the builder's goodwill began to recede like ozone in the age of hairspray. "Mr. Glave," he said at one point, "I need to inform you that I intend to charge a five-thousand-dollar man-agement fee to cover the administrative costs of all your change orders." (I declined to pay it.) To be clear, not all of our blueprint meddling was for the sake of Mother Earth. Seduced by the idea of little luxuries writ large, we blew part of our goodwill budget on reworking the master bath to accommodate a big pedestal-style soaker bathtub. It practically needs a carbon-offset program all of its own.

We ended up with a comfortable, reasonably efficient home, and despite one or two e-mail gunfights with our builder, we're all still talking to one another. Our place will not win any design awards, but it is neither "minimally finished" nor minimally completed, and our view is truly a gasper.

But we are paying the hidden price for our "affordable" house. Although our lot boasts excellent exposure, our home's south side features a near-total lack of glass (we added the only small window—a tiny one in the kitchen). On sunny winter days, we turn on the lights and heat a little earlier in the afternoon than we would otherwise need to. This all-but-windowless wall isn't just inefficient, it's ugly: Our house—which was obviously not designed for its site—greets visitors with a grim expanse of siding, punctuated with little more than a glass door showcasing the cluttered laundry room beyond.

Then there's our electric hot-water heater, which spins the meter day and night. It squats in the crawl space at the extreme opposite end of the house from the fixtures; we run the kitchen-sink faucet for a full minute before we get hot water, squandering endless gallons and kilowatts along the way. The double-glazed windows and doors keep the heat in, but like our Santa Fe swap-outs, they're built with vinyl, which I have recently learned is among the most environmentally hazardous consumer substances on Earth. As for the kitchen cabinets, they were made in the traditional way—with formaldehyde.

Which brings us to the question of indoor air quality. Sustainably designed homes often include a device called a heat-recovery ventilator, which constantly exchanges stale and moist inside air with fresh stuff from the great outdoors—without losing much heat in the process. A pair of small fans working in tandem can completely exchange a large home's inner atmosphere in about three hours while retaining about 70 percent of its precious warmth. The units aren't that expensive; they run a few thousand dollars installed—about the price of a good stretch of granite countertop. But our almost-green home doesn't have one.

Instead, in a nod to the fact that our place is sealed tight against the wet Canadian winter with a few hundred yards of plastic vapor barrier, the builder wired the bathroom fan on the main floor to a programmable timer. It runs for an hour every afternoon, pulling in replacement air from the leaks around our doors and windows. This cool air, of course, trips the electric baseboard heaters. When I showed this setup to an architect friend of mine, he shook his head and grinned, dismissing it as a Mickey Mouse ventilation system. In other words, it doesn't work. The evidence can be found, in winter, on the frames of our upstairs bedroom windows, where mold has begun to colonize the vinyl.

Our present tract home is considerably more efficient than our mid-twentieth-century Santa Fe casa, but for all its boffo insulation and Energy Star appliances, its rainwater-harvesting capabilities and carbon-neutral wood stove, it really isn't keeping us healthy or the planet happy. But it represents the best combination of our intentions, finances, and consciousness at the time. Although green condo and townhouse developments are now finally beginning to crop up here and there, when we built our place three years back, a sustainable home was still very much a custom home. And those were then—and largely remain today—the purview of families more financially solvent than ours.

Now we have a chance to do it right the third time, on a much smaller scale. Although we didn't have a clue about heat-recovery ventilators—this would doubtless have pushed our cranky builder over the edge—we did ask him to pour a small pad foundation in the front yard to one day host a modest writing studio and overnight guest suite.

We didn't have the money to build the studio at the outset, but we could scrape together the $5,300 he quoted us to knock out a design, rough in the utilities, and deposit the concrete inside a fourteen-by-twenty-foot rectangle on the back side of our double carport.

After a year in the house, with the market going haywire, we'd amassed enough home equity to tackle the project. And we both knew instinctively what we wanted to do.

"Love, I've been thinking about the studio," I said to Elle one night in early 2005, as we sat basking in the glow of our ultraefficient Danish woodstove. "Why don't we do it as a really deep-green project?"

"What do you mean?"

"Well, we're going to build it at some point, right? We can't live with that concrete foundation out there forever. Why don't we do what we wanted to do with this place and put ourselves in the driver's seat, really do our homework, and do it right this time, you know?"

"Nice idea, but you're talking about spending a small fortune," Elle replied. "Forget it. We both know green building is for Valhalla," she said, referring to one of Bowen's seven-figure neighborhoods.

"Maybe not," I said. I'd been researching the business case for sustainable design; some studies indicated that a green building could cost as much as 30 percent more than a so-called market building, but depending on how creatively we approached the project, and how much work we put in ourselves, the premium could amount to as little as nil.

"It would be a small project, a chance to do something good and learn the ins and outs on a small scale, with smaller stakes. I could probably handle the general contracting and pitch in on the work."

An orchestra began to swell in the background, and a set of compact-fluorescent floodlights came up as I stepped up to my imaginary podium and sketched out my grand vision—which I was more or less making up as I went along. "Just imagine," I told my rapt audience—Elle and the cat—"this studio could be a kind of green-building petri dish, an opportunity to do everything we wanted to do here in the house but couldn't because we were broke and three thousand miles away and sleep deprived and both on the verge of nervous breakdowns.

It could be our chance to do it right the second, er, I mean, *third* time!"

Elle indulged me. Generally, she and I are very proton and electron, yin and yang, Mars and Venus—what I mean to say is that we bicker. By my calculations, we agree on big life decisions approximately 14 percent of the time. This was one of those rare and precious moments when the planets aligned in our marriage. We agreed, in principle, to go for it.

Meanwhile, just outside, in the dark and the rain, cemented hard up against the back side of the seventeen-thousand-dollar carport where we stationed our nonhybrid suv, a rectangle of concrete anticipated its moment in the sun. With household finances stabilizing—well, sort of—we were ready once again to dive into deep water, albeit this time, we hoped, with far more manageable stakes.

We'd finally be as green as we always wanted to be. We'd stick to our guns from beginning to end. We agreed that the place would be assembled with low-impact, nontoxic materials—sourced as locally as possible. It would require very little energy to heat and light. We'd throw open its doors to the community as a showcase of sustainable building practices, theoretically accessible to the middle class. It would be the most energy-efficient home office on Bowen Island and, perhaps, in Western Canada. And we'd call it the Eco-Shed.

Ah, the blissful naïveté of youth.

2

Crash Course

"Do you *seriously* think we're up for this?" Elle asked one day, as I started digging into my green-building research in earnest. I replied with encouraging noises, but we both already knew the answer: not in the least.

It's easy enough to make a strong case for green building at the scale of, say, a skyscraper. But a home-office studio? We'd more or less committed ourselves to building *something* in the garden a year or so earlier when our builder poured the foundation. Elle's dad had generously given us a carport as a housewarming gift. And we calculated we'd save about five thousand dollars if we had the studio slab poured, adjacent to that carport, at the same time, rather than hiring a truck to pour concrete again later. Although the most sustainable choice would, of course, be to build nothing at all, we didn't want to stare at the concrete box forever. Not only did the Eco-Shed feel like an opportunity to revive once-dashed ecological ambitions, it also began to feel like something of a moral imperative.

But given that I wouldn't be able to realize any economies of scale out there in the yard, I needed to be sure that I had solid reasons for going for the green gusto. Before tapping my precious reserves of time, effort, and money, I needed more than just a strong hunch. More important, I needed to convince a critical but still-skeptical audience—namely, my wife, who manages the household finances.

I didn't have to look too hard for supporting stats. Most green structures are office buildings, and, unsurprisingly, most attempts to study the form focus on how they make money, through energy savings and productivity gains. Although eco-offices may not magically transform miserable white-collar drones into shiny, happy people, evidence is mounting that sustainable buildings make people healthier, more productive, and generally more fun to be around. Indeed, since investigators first flagged sick-building syndrome back in the 1970s, researchers have attempted to nail the connection between indoor environmental quality (IEQ)—not just air circulation, but lighting, desk design, and dozens of other variables—and worker well-being.

If anyone knew the value of IEQ, it was me. Back in 1991, I spent eight months toiling inside a hermetically sealed office tower that still stands today as a case study for how shoddy and careless building design can literally make workers ill. The complex, called Les Terrasses de la Chaudière (the waterfall terraces), is located in Hull, Quebec, just across the river from Canada's Parliament buildings. In 1979, shortly after its first occupants fired up their IBM Selectrics, they began experiencing a variety of ailments, including irritated eyes and upper respiratory tracts.

Follow-up studies proved inconclusive. Well, most of them: "Some of the investigations suggested that flaws in the design and construction of the building were to blame," notes a 1998 University of Calgary environmental design thesis dedicated to the complex. "Examples included decaying food and debris left in air ducts during construction, washroom vents that were not connected to roof vents, and migration of air from the exhaust vents to air intakes."

The moldy sandwiches had allegedly long since been swept from the vents when I began my student internship—which largely involved cranking out press releases about how nicely Canada was treating its aboriginals. But within a month, I contracted one of the most miserable cases of bronchitis of my life. I stayed in bed for ten days, hacking up cups of green and brown phlegm and what must have been several pounds of lung tissue. Of course, my severe upper-respiratory-tract infection was almost certainly a coincidence. It likely had nothing to do with the fact that the receptionists who are probably still employed in the building today unfairly called it "Les Terrasses de la Shoddy Air."

But anyway, all of this research linking health and happiness with workspace was precisely the kind of support I needed to sell my deep-green-building agenda. This was especially true of the "happiness" part, because lately, I had to admit, I hadn't always been a lot of fun to be around. My career was in limbo, and although I loved my kids and cherished the time we had together, the endless papier-mâché projects were starting to wear thin. This studio could be a chance for reinvention, and it could be a good outlet for my relentless ambition and drive. I just needed to convince my wife that this was the way to go. I assembled a few key studies, went through them with a yellow highlighter—the same one Elle used to review our credit card statements ("What is this twenty-five dollars for sluttykay.com?")—and went in to close the sale.

Elle was, in principle, onboard with the idea of the Eco-Shed. She knew it would save energy and reduce emissions, albeit on a tiny scale. The fresh-start concept appealed to her. But as the domestic controller, she'd expressed reservations about the expected price premium. It was time to bring her fully onside. I gathered up my notes and joined her one evening at the kitchen table. She was busy doing what working parents do when the kids finally conk out for the night: drinking red wine and folding heaps of spaceship underwear and pink My Little Pony T-shirts.

"This is why we need to build the studio ultra-green," I told her confidently, reaching for a pair of size-four jeans with permanent grass stains on the knees.

"For one thing, this is going to be my new office, and a deep-green building will make me work harder."

Elle looked at me over the top of her glasses with one of those classic you've-got-to-be-kidding looks. "Huh."

"Listen, I'll have total and precise temperature control right at my fingertips." I turned to a 2003 report prepared by the U.S. Green Building Council and a coalition of California state agencies. The study found that companies offering their employees workstation-specific thermostats watched productivity jump around 7 percent.

"Seven percent?" Silence. "And we'd be spending how much more to build it?"

"OK, maybe it doesn't sound like a lot, but for a Fortune 500 company, that's big coin. For me, um, maybe it's only one extra freelance assignment, a grand or two. But what if it's enough to cover most of a trip down to visit your family for Thanksgiving?" (I mentally congratulated myself on my psychological sparring ability.)

I grinned hopefully and began collating Thomas the Train socks.

"Then there's the ventilation system. You know how it feels stuffy in the house here in the winter, and when we open all the windows in the spring all that pollen blows in?"

No response.

"We'll probably want to have an HRV running in there—a heat-recovery ventilator, with a HEPA filter. The air in the Eco-Shed not only will be fresh but will actually be cleaner than the air outside!"

"I'm skeptical."

"So, according to Lawrence Berkeley National Labs, improved indoor air quality could save U.S. companies $200 billion a year in sick days that would otherwise not be booked. *I'm sick all the time in winter!*"

This was true. My friend Doug used to call it Glave Flu. What if it was poor office air quality doing me in, all this time?

"I can't work when I've got Glave Flu," I said. "That's money lost that I could be earning for the family."

"I see," she said. Our Energy Star–certified dryer buzzed, and I collected a load of whites. I'm a big advocate for doing my homework *and* housework. This was going well.

"Then there's the daylight," I said. My current basement workspace (technically, a small, semi-level patch of rough concrete in the crawl space) didn't offer much natural light. Like all green buildings, the Eco-Shed would need to be flooded with the stuff.

I glanced at my notes. "A 2004 study of spinal surgery patients found that those exposed to bright sunlight experienced less stress and less pain than those in artificially lit environments. You know how stressed out I always am?"

"Correct. And you'll be biting your nails down to the knuckles when you have to start making your Eco-Shed payments. Look, I'm trying to be open-minded, but show me the money. Where's it coming from upfront?"

Damn, the woman had a point. I was almost finished rolling the towels, day-spa style, and was running out of research papers to cite.

"What if you decide to learn French for your job?"

The idea wasn't that far-fetched; Elle works for a federal government agency operating in both of Canada's official languages. French fluency could bump her up a salary bracket.

She gave me that look again.

"Yeah, and what if monkeys fly out of my ass?" she replied.

I was grasping and she knew it. Continuing education wasn't even a remote possibility for either of us at this stage in the game, even if it might spell a small salary raise for her. Actually, it wasn't even on the long-range list of stuff to consider when the kids both finally reach elementary-school age.

"Just hear me out. Say one of us wanted to take a distance ed course; the Eco-Shed would help us nail it. A 2001 study by the Heschong Mahone Group found that students learned 21 percent faster in classrooms with the most daylight compared with classrooms with the least daylight."

"I'm not going to learn French."

"OK, scratch that last one. Listen, this project feels like the right thing to do. One of the reasons this house bums us out— you know, floor boards separating and siding already cracking— is because it's built to the bare-minimum standards."

"We could only afford the bare minimum," she said.

"I know, I know," I replied. "But you know something? The minimum just isn't cutting it anymore. It sucks. We need to start sending the message that we need to do better, try harder, expect more. That's the only way things will ever change. The stakes are just getting too high. If we demand green as the legally required baseline, then the market will provide it, and the price of this stuff will come down."

My yellow-highlighter research didn't move her, but my passion did. By the time we'd filled three baskets with another week's worth of day-care outfits, I had the controller in my back pocket. Complete spousal buy-in. Now, I thought, if we ended up raiding the kids' college savings accounts to get the occupancy permit, at least I could say the decision was both of ours.

My brave green journey was officially underway. Now I needed some advice to get me headed in the right direction.

* * *

In the mid-1970s, in what is widely considered one of North America's most successful urban-revitalization projects, a visionary batch of politicians, planners, and architects parlayed a greasy toxic smear of dilapidated factories on Vancouver's waterfront into a thriving district of studios, theaters, restaurants, and boutiques.

Today it is known as Granville Island, and its crown jewel is a 49,000-square-foot public market, an extravaganza of sights, sounds, and flavors—locally grown wasabi leaves, anyone?—that elevated produce into porn long before Whole Foods styled its first utterly perfect carrot. And just next door to this culinary orgy, in a space above a chocolate factory and within shouting distance of a roaring concrete plant, you'll find a cluttered little loft that is working to help save the world, one blueprint at a time.

It's called the Light House Sustainable Building Centre, and it's a regional magnet for would-be green builders. Part resource library, part outreach operation, the Light House is staffed by gung-ho heating engineers, enthusiastic architects, and scores of young volunteers. The tiny space is crammed with product samples, reference books, and cool architectural models. Walk in off the street with a set of drawings, or even an inkling of an idea sketched on a napkin, and a sustainable-building expert will sit down with you, take a look, and offer advice, for free, on the spot about how to tweak it more to Mother Nature's liking.

One warm Wednesday in August 2006, I unrolled my own blueprints in front of Helen Goodland, the center's executive director. Goodland is a warm and bright expat Brit. Her résumé includes managing Metro Vancouver's green-building initiative and working under local green "starchitect" Peter Busby, who is designing wind-turbine-equipped Wal-Marts.

The bespectacled redhead is as efficient as the buildings she has helped put together. She is refreshingly direct—as many Europeans are. I once asked her for her thoughts on what I felt was a visionary green essay I'd penned for a local magazine, and she'd told me—more or less—that it was crap. But she is also a gifted diplomat, able to comfortably hold the floor at a fundraising reception. She has a touch of headmistress about her, and like me, she doesn't suffer fools gladly.

For all of these reasons, I liked Goodland immensely, especially when, within ten minutes of meeting me, she took all my preconceived notions about sustainable building and tossed them into the blue bin with the Pepsi cans.

The plans before us on the table for Lot 55, as the developer had registered our property, outlined a fourteen-by-twenty-one-room studio—with a small, integrated bathroom and kitchenette—that our spec builder had designed, at our request, for the back side of our double carport. We'd conceived the little structure as a place to work and a spot to house occasional overnight guests. Perhaps we might stash an au pair in there one day.

Like the main house, the studio that so far only existed on paper really had no green qualities. It was drawn and conceived as a miniature satellite of our house, with the same vinyl windows and electric baseboard heaters, separated from the main house by ten feet of dirt and connected to our home via underground pipes and conduit that, at this point, carried neither water nor wires.

After poring over the blueprints and listening patiently for a few minutes to my enthusiastic spiel about what I hoped a redesigned studio would incorporate—cedar shingles split from logs off the beach!—Goodland asked me if I had a builder in mind.

"Well, actually, I was going to serve as the general contractor. I'll run the project, make all the decisions, bring in the trades." I figured that I couldn't exactly learn about green building if someone else were doing it for me.

"You might think carefully about that," she replied. "At some point you are going to find yourself on what we call a critical path—you need to be on-site and anticipate things, and then you may find you need to go to Mexico for a month, and the whole thing stops."

"Well, I can't learn about green building by watching it out the front windows, and I don't want some guy making decisions on my behalf, cutting corners and making compromises that I don't want to make. I mean, I want to think about sourcing a lot of the materials myself ..."

"Let's set aside a discussion of materials for a minute," Goodland said, slipping into headmistress mode. "I would first like to introduce you to the concept of integrated design."

Instantly connecting the dots in my head between "integrated design" and "$250-per-square-foot custom home"—the path Elle and I had concluded wasn't an option—I immediately shut her down.

"We can't afford integrated design!"

"It is not a question of affording it," Goodland patiently replied. "It is a question of process—one that helps you benefit from the choices that you make."

Although it *is* undeniably a question of cost, integrated design, it turns out, lies at the very heart of all green-building projects. It's an innovative way of thinking about what structures are and how they go together, rooted in the idea that a home is more than just a box full of pipes, wires, and fixtures. Instead, it is a living system made up of individual pieces—heating, cooling, electrical, plumbing—that all work together and play off one another. Tweak one bit, and it tweaks the others.

In conventional construction—the kind that assembled my house—each of a building's systems are designed and installed in relative isolation. An architect or designer drafts the plans, and the client signs off and hands them to a general contractor, who rotates them in turn through a long string of subcontractors— excavators, framers, plumbers, electricians, insulation installers, drywallers, tilers—each of whom comes and goes and does his solo thing. Lines are carefully drawn to preserve accountability and liability. Turf is defended. A plumber may notice a way to improve the arrangement of the home's hydronic heat system but more often than not keeps his mouth shut. And it doesn't matter to the builder. He won't be paying the heating bills. He's working for a fixed contract price, and even an hour or two of time spent thinking about how to improve the place is money out of his pocket. The only efficiencies that interest spec builders are those that allow them to assemble the home to code more cheaply without the client's noticing. To those guys, the whole concept of integrated design is a massive time suck, and time is money.

But had we gone through an integrated design process, we'd almost certainly have windows on our south wall. We'd have a hot-water tank close to the faucets and a ventilation system that actually ventilates. Integrated design aims to head off blunders like these before they happen. It tears down long-ago ingrained turf walls by bringing together all of a project's stakeholders to share ideas and experiences at the beginning of the process. Insulation contractors schmooze with framers. The heating and cooling people throw ideas at the roofers and together run innovative solutions past the building inspector, who is theoretically sitting right over there.

This kind of workshop, known as a charrette, encourages cross-pollination and experience sharing to scrutinize variables such as efficiency, flexibility, cost, livability, and environmental impact. It throws a light on all the things that make a building greener and more livable. And it's Helen Goodland's first prescription for my little 280-square-foot Eco-Shed.

So why, then, do I want to crawl under the nearest formaldehyde-free fiberboard desk?

* * *

The truth is, although I am all about innovative ideas, I may not be the best person to oversee a project that involves intensive collaboration and team building. Like many journalists, I'm not much of a joiner, and I'm deeply suspicious of touchy-feely "visioning processes." Put a group of smart people together in a room to build consensus and work through a problem, and I am the jerk at the table who keeps checking his watch and finishing other people's sentences for them. There's a fine line between skeptic and cynic, and I have spent most of my life straddling it.

Then there's my headstrong character. For better or worse—and usually it's the latter—my internal tachometer has always registered in the red, a fact that explains why a former boss of mine once gave me the nickname Turbo. It was the late nineties, the dot-com heyday, and I found myself leading a team in the worst possible enabling environment—the newsroom of a technology wire service. I was on the job and in the chair each weekday by 6:30 a.m., and for the next twelve hours, I pretty much only left the room when my bladder ordered me to. I'd assign a story to a reporter, then go over and casually check on his or her progress thirty-five minutes later. If news broke on Saturday night, I'd wake up my staff Sunday morning to publish our piece.

To some extent, this situation was our competitive reality, but I took it to the next level. My boss loved me, but he might as well have hired an alcoholic to tend bar. The pace was simply unsustainable. On an infamous early date with the woman who would later become my wife, I fell asleep in the middle of the movie, allegedly snoring with my mouth wide open. There I was, sawing logs in the balcony in the third act of *Citizen Kane*.

I left that job but didn't slow down. My subsequent supervisor, in an annual performance review that will haunt me forever, gently informed me I was scaring my colleagues.

"Some people in this office put out about 60 or 75 percent of effort, try to puff it up to make it look like 100 and hope nobody notices," he said. "But you operate at the other extreme. You put out 125 percent of effort—and don't get me wrong, it's all great, industrious, high-quality stuff—but to those around you, it comes across more like 150."

The meeting was a heart-to-heart character assassination that concluded with a salary raise. "You are a very good editor," the boss man told me, following the management script of always prefacing a negative with a positive. "And you could be a great editor. What's holding you back is this manic energy that you broadcast. It kind of freaks people out."

This is what I grappled with as I launched into a construction project that might well prove the trickiest test of my murky leadership skills to date. I would need to build a team and motivate and inspire my partners—some of whom would doubtless be, at various stages, volunteers bribed with pizza and beer. I would need to patiently research and evaluate cutting-edge techniques and materials and listen to others with an open mind. Basically, I would need to not freak out.

Although the design details had yet to be sorted out, the endgame would be a studio that would be about as far away from plug-and-play construction as one could get. It would be a time- and money-intensive project. And, owing to the vagaries of my stay-at-home-dad lifestyle and my compulsive need to push the envelope, I would need to do it in about eight months for about—gulp—$75,000, which was about all my spouse and loan officer would let me have.

Having just built, with the best of intentions, a house that didn't turn out to be as green as I would have liked, I was giving myself another opportunity to leave a lighter residential footprint on Planet Earth. The new place could serve as a new-model-home-in-miniature, the toast of my community. Perhaps the mayor would attend the opening!

And perhaps—if the credit union didn't foreclose on us, if my nimby neighbors didn't kill the project before it started, if the day care didn't keep sending the kids home with pinkeye, if I didn't push my wife too close to the edge—if all these things *didn't* happen, well then, the Eco-Shed might prove a chance for another kind of transformation. Hey, if a stressed-out, socially challenged, stay-at-home dude like me could pull off a gig like this, so could anyone. There might still be hope for the man called Turbo. There might still be hope for us all.

Provided, that is, I could find an architect who wouldn't strangle me. And here, again, Headmistress Goodland came to my rescue.

"To be perfectly frank, your project is probably too small for many architects to bother with," she said. "You'll probably want someone young, just out of school." Someone who could use a gig like my little studio to kickstart his or her green-design career. That someone, she concluded, was Heather Choi (not her real name), who had come out of university back east less than a year before, who had been toiling part-time at the Light House, and who seemed to genuinely understand green design.

"Heather comes with my blessing and heartiest support," Goodland e-mailed me. I was off.

3

My Suburban Sarcophagus

There really was nothing wrong with the modest poured-slab foundation jutting off the back side of the carport on Lot 55. It was doing its job, waiting patiently to host a small structure that would one day be built atop it—a cozy little retreat that would provide its owners with peace and quiet and their overnight friends and family with warmth and privacy. A dozen-odd stainless-steel anchor bolts protruded at regular intervals around its perimeter, ready to accept a set of completed two-by-six exterior walls that would be built flat on the ground, then raised and slotted down upon them. One day, someone would then drop large washers over those bolts, then ratchet down a series of nuts, permanently tying the new structure to its concrete mass and, by extension, the bedrock that lay below.

Wires would be threaded through the stubs of orange plastic conduit that poked up out of the concrete, bringing the building lifelines of electricity, TV cable, and telephone. Plumbing fixtures—a toilet, a shower, a couple of sinks—would be connected to the flexible black plastic water piping that presently dangled in a loose coil. Those same fixtures would also be tied into the various black plastic drainpipes that protruded from the concrete where our builder had sketched out a bathroom and kitchenette.

As the slab embarked on its second West Coast winter without benefit of a protective shell, it began to show the effects of the weather. A green stain of algae bloom marked a low spot on its otherwise dead flat, matte-gray surface. Rust ate into the nails that had been hammered flush around its exposed vertical sides. Sun and rain disintegrated much of the duct tape that sealed off the conduit; kids had picked off the rest like scabs.

If the slab did indeed have a soul, as it does in my twisted imagination, it might hope that people would one day walk just above its hulking mass in the snug studio that it would eventually support. Perhaps they'd make themselves a cup of tea and look out the window across the fjord to the steep slopes of the Britannia Range. The sun would drop down in the west, throwing the six-mile-long shadow of our island on the forested purple mountainside across the channel. Then the guests would tuck themselves into bed.

The slab knew it was technically perfect. It dutifully complied with the relevant sections of the British Columbia Building Code. All it needed to feel whole was a truckload of materials and a skilled set of hands laboring for a few weeks with saws and hammers.

What it couldn't possibly know was that for all its strengths and usefulness, it was in precisely the wrong place.

The foundation extended twelve feet from the back side of my carport, which occupied the front of my property. Our parcel touched the street in a narrow wedge that pointed due south. An eight-foot wall, an asphalt-shingled roof, and a six-foot-wide sport-utility vehicle blocked the slab's sunny southern exposure. The only warming rays that would land on the future site of my Eco-Shed spilled around from the west and the east in summer—the time of year they were neither wanted nor needed. In winter, the slab lingered in shadow.

This was a problem, because Helen Goodland at the Light House Sustainable Building Centre had suggested I dispense with baseboard heaters. On her advice, there would be no pro-pane fireplace in the corner of my Eco-Shed, no miniature forced-air furnace. The plan was to warm this space for the most part with food—transformed via human digestion into radiant body heat—and good old-fashioned nuclear fusion, available locally, for free, as sunlight. It would be designed as a passive-solar house, a superinsulated structure warmed with ordinary old Sol and so-called process loads, which is to say the heat coming out of my laptop computer and the lights and the heat coming off me.

"Design it to reduce the heating requirements right from the beginning," Goodland had said at our meeting back in the sum-mer. "And that means, instead of having to spend four thousand dollars on some kind of heating system, you are going to shift those costs to your building envelope."

"So, instead of spending money on a furnace, spend it on the walls and windows?" I asked.

"Exactly," she replied. "It's called cost-shifting. And think carefully about those windows. Go for a smaller, but better, window. A giant, cheap one means you have to replace it that much quicker."

Go for a smaller window. This idea was difficult for me to get my head around. Years of reading modern, hip architectural magazines had convinced me that the only appropriate response to an epic view like the one outside my future Eco-Shed is a wall of floor-to-ceiling glass showing it off. Like everyone else in my neighborhood—nay, on this continent—I wanted to bring the outside in. Now I was supposed to specify weenie wittle windows? Perhaps I should install a porthole. I could always get up and peer out whenever I wanted to look at the bitchin' ocean-and-mountain panorama that Elle and I had mortgaged ourselves up the yin-yang to acquire.

"At the absolute minimum you want Energy Star–rated windows," Goodland continued, citing sustainable living's answer to the *Good Housekeeping* Seal of Approval. "But the most important thing is how tightly that window is sealed."

"Right," I said. "I want the space between the two panes to be purged with nitrogen, or whatever."

"Well, everyone has been saying you need argon-filled windows and, of course, you do—but only if you have a totally sealed unit. You need to ask the manufacturer what the percentage of air leakage is. If they can't tell you, don't buy their windows. You want it around 2 percent or less per year. Some leak as much as 5 percent."

The reason air leakage is so important is because it is, in fact, heat leakage. And when the gales of November come early to the Pacific Northwest, warmth will be my Eco-Shed's most precious commodity.

I later clicked around a few major window manufacturer Web sites. Not one company bragged about its air leakage values. According to Goodland, this is because these window firms—those familiar brands that got that way by heavily investing in magazine-and-television marketing campaigns—will likely need to completely retool their production lines to reach a new level of performance. They are reluctant to do so, reasonably enough; so far, nobody is asking them to.

Goodland also suggested I hire an engineer to run a computer simulation of the Eco-Shed's heating loads—a digital analysis of how much warmth my little space will need, how much glass will help the sun give it to me, how much will come from secondary sources (like my laptop computer), when too many giant picture windows will start working against me, and so on.

"The study is going to be based on your occupancy, how often you are going to be in there, what temperature swings you are comfortable with," Goodland said. "I mean, you'll need to ask yourself, 'Am I OK with putting a sweater on now and then?' Everyone has become conditioned to think they have to be able to walk around in their underwear twenty-four hours a day to be comfortable, and it's just not the case."

The greener-thans are forever crowing about the hedonistic pleasures that could come from the sustainable life—hey, sorting tin cans is fun, just like cycling to work in February, right? I always smelled a rat in this feel-good jingoism. I knew there would be some significant lifestyle trade-offs in my future, and sure enough, here is the first: in our post-permafrost tomorrowland, it seems I won't be able to dance around my writing studio in the middle of the night, wearing boxers and playing air guitar to the amplified wailings of Bob Seger.

"I think I'd be all right with wearing a sweater now and then," I said.

In truth, everything Goodland said made sense. She wasn't ordering me to shrink the windows. She was telling me to get the best panes I could possibly afford and carefully plan their size and location to maximize heat gain in the right places, minimize it in others, and stop warmth from going in the other direction as much as possible. Since most of a building's energy goes into heating and hot water, and after sunset much of it literally goes out the window, Goodland was prescribing an Eco-Shed that would capture warmth and keep it inside its thick, puff-stuffed walls. She was suggesting a small, well-planned, ultraefficient space that would, as much as possible, heat itself.

The key to pulling off all this wizardry, Goodland explained, would be some kind of thermal mass inside the studio that would absorb the sun's rays. By this she meant a dense, heat-absorbing surface. A brick wall, perhaps, or one made of stacked and mortared stone, or a concrete floor. The idea is to invite the sun to soak into something big and dense and solid, a surface that can warm up, or charge, throughout the day, then slowly radiate heat back into the room at night.

"If you have a very efficient structure, you don't need a lot of heat," said Goodland. "You just need to keep it in there. You need to keep it at a constant temperature."

Evidently, the secret to combating global warming is to replicate, inside our homes, the very process that drives it: the greenhouse effect. Winter sunlight will theoretically pour in through the Eco-Shed's windows, where it will bake my thermal mass—the exposed concrete floor, perhaps—which at night will then slowly release the heat back into the room, where it has nowhere else to go. Instead of having a furnace cycle on and off until dawn, creating sharp peaks and valleys on a temperature line graph, I will be able to flatten those highs and lows. I'll even it up.

This was all fascinating and completely logical. But there were a couple of snags. First, it rains rather often on Bowen Island in the chilly seasons. During the particularly gray month of January 2006, water dumped out of the skies and onto my rock every single day, around the clock. Passive solar only works when the sun is out, right?

Right, but the question was moot. Because second, whenever the winter sun did climb reluctantly into the sky, there would be no south-facing glass on my Eco-Shed to greet it, since a solid wall stood in the way: the back side of the timber-framed carport. Essentially, this oversized structure was robbing us of the rays we would need to warm our low-emissions Office of Tomorrow.

In short, we'd committed the front half of Lot 55 to suburban infrastructure, and we were already paying the price. I found myself emotionally entangled in both the vehicle, which I felt less and less comfortable driving, and the timber-framed protective shell that housed it. Although my father-in-law had hinted that he didn't exactly think the carport was an award-winning design, I felt nervous about dismantling it for fear of offending him. Especially since, well, he's not yet quite onboard with this whole anthropogenic global warming thing.

Padre has a wacky, eccentric sense of humor. He's intelligent and kind. He's a doting grandpa. Like me, he likes outdoor adventure. I once worked my magazine connections to secure him a couple of wholesale-priced kayaks, a few pairs of walk-in-water shoes, and the occasional score of an LED headlamp or a pair of sunglasses. But on some things we just don't see eye to eye. He's a dedicated Republican, a successful businessman, and an excellent pilot—please don't tell the FAA, but he once briefly let me take the controls on a run down the Rio Grande Gorge, an unforgettable thrill. Recently, he beamed me a Photoshop image of a trio of polar bears roasting a penguin on a spit. Subject line: "The Real Cause of Global Warming!" Another of Padre's e-mails found evidence of our sweltering planet in a series of annotated *Playboy* centerfolds. (Trust me, you don't want to know.)

So the carport was a tricky subject. If I took it apart to afford my passive-solar studio its critical access to sunshine, would I dismantle our relationship as well?

Setting aside the question of Padre for a moment, in my mind the carport ultimately represented, on a microscale, what author James Howard Kunstler calls the "psychology of previous investment." Kunstler, author of the harrowing peak-oil primer *The Long Emergency*, argues that the biggest obstacle to the serious and inevitable overhaul of our vehicle-centric environment is the simple fact that it's already there. "Having poured so much of our late-twentieth-century wealth into this living arrangement—this Happy Motoring utopia—we can't imagine letting go of it, or substantially reforming it," he writes. And he's right. The carport was there—a hulking, ugly, and uninspired asphalt roof on stilts. It allowed us to unload our children and groceries in the depths of a West Coast winter without getting soaked. But when we sat down to itemize its upsides, the list stopped there.

* * *

Soon enough, in early November Heather Choi and I were having a fish-and-chips lunch at a restaurant in Horseshoe Bay—the scruffy village where our ferry docks on the mainland just across the channel. Wearing a long black overcoat, her bleached-blonde hair in a short bob, my green-building researcher was a bit goth, if perhaps also uncertain. She invited me to confront the hard realities of my slab, which despite my best efforts at denial, was still in the wrong place if it were to host a passive-solar Eco-Shed. We'd decided to warm the slab with pipes of hot water, heated by a source still open to discussion. But one big problem remained.

"Your in-slab hot-water tubing system—that can give you about 50 percent of your heating needs," Choi said. "And passive design, just orienting the building the right way, can give you about 40 percent, so long as the sun is shining. So you are pretty much set, right?"

"But passive houses need southern exposure. And your vehicle is …" She paused. "Sort of in the way."

"Perhaps we could reverse the spaces," I suggested. "What if we park the car where the foundation slab is now and build the Eco-Shed in the carport?"

That configuration—essentially, we'd flip the structure around—intrigued both of us because it would hide the car from the street. But it was also flawed. The angles were all wrong. The slab was more than a foot above grade, so we'd need to bring in fill and build a curved and sloping driveway that would come in around the side of the present carport, then hook sharply to the left. There was precious little maneuvering room, and besides, what space there was was off-limits. Elle and I had planned to put a garden there, including a small orchard of dwarf fruit trees. To replace this future culinary Eden with a curving SUV ramp—the sort of thing you'd encounter in a six-story parking garage—well, it just didn't seem to fit the story line.

At the same time, I wasn't yet ready to tear out the studio slab and start over someplace else. Cursed as I was with the psychology of previous investment, I didn't want to waste the $5,300 we'd already spent on the concrete, not to mention the considerable carbon dioxide emissions that went into making it and getting it there—the sum total of hidden resources and impacts known as its embodied energy. Paving over the planned orchard to build an Eco-Shed seemed absurd. But at the moment, it appeared to be the only way to reach our savvy new passive-solar goals without taking an excavator to the carport. We were already paying for the lack of sun in our existing house in the form of higher utility bills. My Eco-Shed would be different.

In the end, I couldn't bear to throw away the concrete foundation. We would have to build the ramp, I resolved. But I would once again need to secure that elusive spousal buy-in.

This time, academic research papers would be of no use to me whatsoever. But I had a plan. First, I'd welcome Elle home from her exhausting hour-and-a-half commute with a kiss and a smile. I'd take her coat and oversized backpack, put up her feet, pour her a glass of chilled British Columbia pinot gris, and surround her with her adoring children. Then I'd gently introduce the idea of converting our future garden and outdoor living space into a sharply curved sloping driveway, perhaps with little guardrails and reflective striping around the outer edges.

I didn't even get as far as the kiss. My beloved called me from her packed-to-the-gills express bus, seeking an update on the Eco-Shed project. Instead of keeping my mouth shut, I unwisely began blabbing out the idea. What if we traded the two spaces, I suggested, before gingerly outlining the scheme's vehicular challenges.

I'd failed to follow my former boss man's policy of always prefacing a negative with a positive, so I gamely tacked a bit on the end: "We could unload our groceries that much closer to the house."

There comes a time in every marriage when wrong words are spoken at the wrong time, and in the wrong way. In my household, this seems to happen every few days or so. It had just happened again.

"Does Heather understand that this is our *garden*?" Elle said, her voice rising like the waters around the tiny island nation of Tuvalu.

I pictured her fellow commuters swiveling their ears in her direction. "Would she want *her* front yard to be a driveway? That's the sunniest part of our whole property! That's where we are going to hang out. That is where we will *grow our vegetables*!"

Then she got to what she really thought: "You are making the studio the number-one priority above all else, and you know what? It isn't."

She hung up. The suv launching ramp was officially off the table. We had not yet begun the project, and I had clearly fumbled one of my golden rules of green: Do not alienate your family or friends.

My buddies were already starting to feel a little awkward around me. The day I shared my Grand Green plans with them, they started apologizing for all the brown stuff they still involved themselves in. And at the same time, they quietly started holding me to a higher standard.

I can offer two examples. The first is my film-biz Pal, Cam. Recently, he built himself a small woodshed. It is a fine, sturdy structure, and Cam was justifiably proud of his work. "But it's not green at all!" he confessed. Indeed, he built it with pressure-treated lumber containing copper, a fungicide, some ammonia, and an insecticide. Personally, I'd have gone with cedar, the oil of which acts as a natural preservative. But Cam wanted his wood-shed to more steadfastly resist the inevitable creep of moss, mold, and time, so he went with the chemicals. Fine, go for it, it's a free world, whatever.

Far from questioning Cam's choices, I went out of my way to offer nothing but admiration for his project. In fact, I reminded him that I have a couple of posts of pressure-treated wood sunk into my own backyard, which I installed before I knew any better. But it wasn't enough. "Really, there's nothing green about the thing," Cam reiterated.

I did my best to assure him I didn't think any less of him or his shed. "Hey, if you take the long view, it *is* green," I recall telling him, "because after all, it's going to last forever. Durability is green." But he kept atoning his sins. Eventually, all I could do was sneak away.

Then there were the sealskin slippers that I recently bought my wife for her birthday. (Quick aside to Paul Watson et al: Please route all hate mail, ticking parcels, blood-filled balloons, etc., through my agent, Vanessa. Thanks.) I mail-ordered the slippers from a craftsperson who lives and works in an isolated Newfoundland fishing village. They are warm and comfortable, and 100 percent of my money went directly into the hands of a local, small-scale artisan toughing it out in a deeply depressed regional economy. I obviously have my own feelings about certain issues that don't neatly align with the green stereotype. Most of our friends good-naturedly gave us a hard time when they heard about the slippers, but others were clearly horrified with what they saw as an ethical disconnect and a double standard. "Wait, those are made with *seal*?!" scolded one of them. "I thought you guys were environmentalists!"

The truth is, the moment you take your life off autopilot—the moment you begin leading by example—you essentially start to tinker with the social order. A few interesting dynamics may emerge as a result. First, in a kind of self-defense mechanism, some might begin holding you to a higher moral standard. Once you publicly embrace green, there's little wiggle room for the occasional Starbuck's latte, McDonald's french-fry binge, or, heaven forbid—dollop of Cool Whip. (These occasional nobody's-perfect indulgences become hypocrisies.)

In an effort to process your new value system, your peeps might fall back on stereotype and expect you to adopt a specific schedule of beliefs and behaviors—a policy platform, if you will—that leaves little room for individual interpretation. (See above re: seal skin.) Eventually, if you rise high enough and begin to threaten other people's way of life, they may also try to punch holes in your green armor—witness the Republican attack on Al Gore's home from a couple of years back.

Eventually, the acceptable norms will evolve, and every one of us will discover that transformational change isn't an all-or-nothing proposition, but rather a dog's breakfast of compromises and personal discoveries. But until then, keep smiling, and keep praising the pesticide-marinated woodsheds in your life, wherever they may lie.

* * *

The following week, Heather Choi and I stood in my front yard, contemplating the fate of a foundation that was barely two years old. It was perfectly serviceable for an energy-sucking twentieth-century studio but nearly useless for the High-Performance Home Office of Tomorrow. Even if we *could* somehow get around the monolith's blocked southern exposure, I'd just made another unfortunate discovery: there was no foam insulation beneath it. Any heat we could pump into the slab would be lost as much to the bedrock below as to the room above.

We had to decide whether this foundation would stay and live out its intended purpose—or die under the steel teeth of a backhoe bucket.

"I think we have to deal with our mistakes," offered Choi. "We should take responsibility for this slab. It's not perfect, but it still deserves to live. I mean, what reason do we really have to get rid of it?"

She gestured through the dividing wall to the pad where we parked our SUV. We had tossed around the idea of slicing a strip off the edge of the carport, reducing the size of the studio, and leaving a narrow parking space off to the side, hard up against a rock wall. "Over there, there's a reason to remove some of it—we need space for the car—but demolishing this foundation would be destructive."

"Well, it's ugly," I said, looking over a mass of concrete that offered only slightly more charm than the rust-streaked sarcophagus keeping the radiation safely inside Chernobyl. "Aesthetics is one reason to get rid of it. There's also safety. If we just leave it here, my kids will continue to play on it. They slip on the slick concrete when it's wet and fall off the edges."

"But we can't just tear things down that we don't like, right?" Choi said. "That is the lesson of urban development."

She thought over our dilemma for a moment or two longer.

"Unless we have a substantial reason, like we can't get access back here or whatever, then we should deal with it."

"OK," I lied.

Then, from Choi, a caveat: "I might be changing my mind."

"I wouldn't blame you," I jumped in. "I want to erase it. I want a chance to start fresh and do it right the second time. We can reuse as much material as we can from the existing structure, like the timber frame, maybe the sheathing. I see the slab hampering our goals, not just esthetic goals; it becomes this thing that we have to incorporate in some way into our high-performance building."

"But isn't architecture a tool for dealing with these things?" Choi asked. "It's not just about a clean slate; it's about assessing the environment. I am not saying we are definitively going to keep it, but we have to critically assess that it does have some value, even just in the fact that it's there.

"This slab is the history of your place," she added. "It is *here*."

I wrestled with the prospect that this fourteen-by-twenty-foot perimeter footing—filled with sand and iced with four inches of smooth concrete—held any level of heritage value. If preserving it meant archiving a moment in the history of Lot 55, I didn't want anything to do with it. It was the ugly product of my pre-evolutionary thinking. It symbolized another time in my life, way back two years ago, when it didn't matter where the sun's rays landed or what lay in their way; when it was no big deal to skip the under-slab insulation—even if I'd known enough to ask for it—because there would be a little electric baseboard heater in there blinking on and off and keeping the place within the "comfort zone."

Today the slab, and the carport attached to it, was an expensive mistake, an emotionally charged installation. Every time I looked at it and tried to picture whatever Band-Aid solution we came up with to deal with it—a mosaic-tile raised patio?—I would wish I hadn't been such a dummkopf.

As Choi and I stood there, I watched my preschooler Sabrina, who had emerged from the house and the fleeting distraction of the video I'd put on to keep her busy. She picked through the rubble surrounding the slab, looking for rusty nails and staples, knowing that I would pay her a shiny dime for each one that she found—my anti-tetanus bounty program. "Here you go, Dad, I found four more," she declared. "How many coins is that?"

"That's forty cents," I told her. "Good work."

"Is that enough for the Playmobil guinea-pig set?"

"Not quite, sweets; better keep looking."

Watching her, I realized I shouldn't be so hard on myself. When this thing was poured, we were just doing the best we could do. We had kids even tinier and more demanding than they were now. We were profoundly tired and in the thick of what our investment adviser described as "a life phase characterized by constrained income." And so we'd forgone custom building in the name of out-of-the-box pricing. There was no integrated-design charrette on Lot 55. Even going the route we did, we ended up spending more than we could afford. The carport was an add-on, the studio space an afterthought.

I'm just glad we didn't go ahead and build the whole thing then. Had we done so, my mistake would've been far more complicated to reckon with. I'd be retrofitting for the second or third time, throwing the proverbial roll of weatherstripping into the junipers all over again. Under this light, I was happy to take a backhoe to the slab. Perhaps I could donate the broken-up concrete to an artificial reef society.

Choi brought me back from my daydream, puncturing my angst-balloon with a note of encouragement. "The trick is to just grab onto those things that you can solve and move forward," she said cheerily. "Then the other things will start to make sense."

In my head, I'd resolved at least one thing. To start fresh with my Eco-Shed, I was going to do with this two-year-old slab foundation what I'd secretly dreamed of doing to my old carbon-spewing house back in Santa Fe.

I was going to tear it down.

4

A Private Green

W e didn't move to our island specifically to pursue a greener life. If we had really wanted to shrink our family's residential and transportation footprint, our woodsy rock with its funky little village would be flat-out the wrong place to go. Instead, we'd have moved into a different kind of forest—the one made of concrete and green glass that is spreading like invasive bamboo across Vancouver's skyline. We would be downtown in a high-rise condo.

Big cities like the one on my doorstop realize tremendous efficiencies of energy and resources simply by packing people tightly together. According to a recent Urban Land Institute study, if the United States shifted just 60 percent of new development to compact growth—mixed-use, walkable neighborhoods— by 2030, the land of the free could prevent the release of about 85 million tons of CO_2 per year. Meanwhile, a 2006 *Journal of Urban Planning and Development* study found that suburban-style development produces two to two and a half times more greenhouse gases per capita than the high-density urban variety.

That's because suburbs, bedroom communities, and charming semirural towns like mine not only suck more energy for heat and power but also usually require commuting—and, by extension, cars.

In 2006, the median sales price for a detached home on my island was $719,000, a fact that explains why between Monday and Friday, hundreds of sleepy wage slaves don heels and suits and migrate downtown. In a private vehicle in the early morning, the commute takes about forty-five minutes, including the ferry ride. Elle makes the trek three times a week and works two days from home. On travel mornings, she usually catches a ride downtown from car-commuter buddies she meets up with on the boat. But inevitably, she takes a packed bus back the other way—an often-suffocating public-transit adventure that, door-to-door, consumes just slightly under two full hours and an immeasurable quantity of life force. It is not sustainable in any respect; we know it, and we struggle with it every day.

The greener-thans have a boilerplate response to solving this emissions and exhaustion angst: "Move closer to your job." And around metro Vancouver, at least, many are doing just that. In recent years, in a reverse-migration pattern still somewhat unique in North America, thousands of British Columbians have passed over, or sold off, detached suburban homes or townhouses for one- or two-bedroom aeries in downtown Vancouver. In doing so, these new urbanites have effectively erased a daily slog that, in this region, averages an hour a day.

It seems a small number of us are drawing the same conclusions as the Washington, D.C.–based Center for Housing Policy, which recently concluded that for every dollar a working American family saves on housing costs by moving to more affordable suburbs, seventy-seven cents are spent on transportation. A number of suburbanites—nobody really knows how many—are doing the math and opting out of the gridlock. They're eBaying Grandma's silver tea service, emptying the closets, swapping the Expedition for a Smart Car or a shared car, and embracing compact urban living in a town blessed with miles of safe seawalls, greenbelts, and parks, plus excellent community centers and libraries. It is this people-friendly urban fabric that led the research arm of *The Economist* to declare the sparkling city on my doorstep the most livable in the world for two years running.

It's a nice eco-utopia they have going over there, but unfortunately, it's not for us.

Like tens of thousands of other young families, we can't afford it. We have two children and 1.5 incomes, and if not now, eventually each of those kids will need his or her own door to retreat behind. There aren't any three-bedroom condos or townhouses in downtown Vancouver for less than what we're paying now— even if we backed out the car and commuting expenses. We'd end up constantly in each other's faces, frantically hustling for work, endlessly squabbling over the organic-grocery delivery bill. Then there's our baggage. We could throw the world's biggest garage sale, and we couldn't possibly cram our lives into that compact a space. Sure, we'd be greener, but we'd probably be in counseling, too.

For all their low-footprint goodness, our cities are neither appealing nor affordable to middle-class families. One child is fine. But have a second, or third, and unless you operate at the far-upper-end of the economic scale, the system kicks you out to Big Box land.

* * *

That's what I thought, at least, until I met Oscar Flechas and his wife, Eliana Castillo. They live with their three children in an elegant, modern, and comfortable condo on the nineteenth floor of a tower in the very heart of the city. He is an architect with his own one-man practice in an office on their building's lower levels. She's a physician in the HIV ward at a nearby hospital. They have a quiet three-and-a-half-year-old girl, a boisterous two-year-old boy—both attend day care about eight blocks away—and an infant who was barely two months old when I went to visit them two weeks before Christmas.

I tracked them down because I wanted to find out just how much living space a young family really needs and what life might be like were we to swap the trees and forests for concrete. Our place is just over eighteen hundred square feet— and now that our house is built and we live within its walls, I am eating humble pie. We could easily have made do with less.

But how much less? Could we squeeze into a tiny condo and still be as happy as we are now, or perhaps more so?

"You should go see these friends of mine," a media-biz crony of mine had suggested. "They've got three kids, and they live in a pretty small place downtown."

The first thing that hit me when I stepped inside the front door of the Flechas-Castillo home was the view—an unobstructed, jaw-dropping floor-to-ceiling spread of sparkling glass towers and soaring mountains beyond. Perhaps it was this grand buzzing panorama, perhaps it was the white walls bathed in natural light, but the place didn't feel cramped.

Then it dawned on me. They didn't have any stuff. Like me, Flechas and Castillo have children under the age of five. Transferring my domestic reality onto theirs, I'd expected banks of knotty-pine Ikea storage units erupting with learn-to-read DVDs, Tonka™ trucks, and various flavors of Dora the Explorer™ officially licensed merchandise. I anticipated racks of neon Play-Doh™ activity sets, tubs of Brio™ train track, perhaps a portable crib jammed into a galley kitchen, dishes stacked in the sink, little handprints on the windows, yogurt on the walls …

Not only was the place spotless, but it was also practically empty. I suspect they prepared for my arrival by jamming all their crap into some far-off storage locker. "Where is all your toddler infrastructure?" I demanded.

"It's called editing," Castillo said proudly. "A new toy comes in; an old one is given away."

I know something about editing, but I also know how kids attract stuff, how they get attached to it, how they can defend it with guilt and hissy fits that make even the most patient and loving parents long for the days of the wooden spoon.

"Wow, that's hard-core. It makes sense, but it must be tough to be that ruthless. So, how much space do you have here?" I asked them.

"This whole place is 659 square feet," said Flechas. Good Lord, I thought, that's just over twice the size of the Eco-Shed! And there are *five* of them in here!

"How's that working for you?"

"Sometimes it's a challenge, but we love it," said Flechas. "It's very freeing to have less stuff."

"We keep what we use," added Castillo. "We keep what we enjoy. We keep what we like."

And for the most part, they kept it out of sight. Flechas had renovated their two-bedroom apartment before they moved in five years back to maximize every square inch. It was one long rectangle: the center section incorporated the kitchen, a small bathroom, dining and living areas. Off either end was a tiny bedroom, one with an en suite bathroom. But there was no clutter anywhere. The tops of the kitchen cabinets were all but deserted. A wall-mounted shelf in the kids' bedroom displayed three or four toys but was mostly empty.

Then the magician revealed his trickery. A set of built-in drawers in the second bedroom appeared to be shallow, until Flechas slid one open. Cleverly, they extended right through the wall behind them, where they tucked inside the bench of a built-in kitchen table on the other side. ("Those ten centimeters inside the wall—we knew we wanted to use them," Castillo explained.) Back in the main room, Dad pointed out a miniature wooden-cube coffee table. Tugging at its sides, he pulled it open to reveal a pair of children's chairs and a couple of drawers, each stocked with paste, crayons, and construction paper.

While most nouveau-greens think about reducing their footprint, here was a family maximizing every square inch.

"Did you show him the baby's crib?" Castillo asked her husband.

The two older kids slept on a twin trundle bed—one half slid under the other—but I'd assumed the infant bunked with his parents. Oscar led me back into the second bedroom, bent down, and extracted a long floor-level drawer from the wall. It contained a small fleece-covered foam mattress. "When the new one came along," he explained, "we realized we needed to buy ourselves another year in this place. So we came up with this."

At that moment, I realized I was witnessing the very frontier of downtown family living in North America: *the baby slept in a drawer.*

"Admittedly, this is a bit extreme," said Flechas, "but this is how we are getting through the next year. Then we will need to find something a little bigger."

"How much bigger?"

"The next apartment that I have been looking at seriously is 795 square feet."

Flechas and Castillo had one more child than Elle and I did, they very likely made more money than we did, yet they figured they needed less than half of our current living space. It just didn't add up. They must have been sugarcoating their life for me. This kind of a setup just couldn't be so easy. When the rain pours down all winter long, they must fight in this shoebox like cats and dogs.

"Don't you feel like you are making all these sacrifices?" I asked, "living on top of each other like this, just to avoid a commute, just to live downtown?"

"Because the space is so small, we don't spend a lot of time here," explained Flechas. "We live our life inside a nine-block radius—that's as far as the day care is. We walk everywhere. It is so simple. Granville Island public market—boom, it's right there. There are three community centers nearby. We have ten parks within a five-block radius. They know us very well at the library."

The family does not own a minivan or suv. Instead, they subscribe to a car-sharing co-op. For a monthly fee, they have access to a small fleet of vehicles—everything from subcompacts to pickups—that are tracked by a Web site and Google Maps. They log on, locate the nearest wheels, and walk over to drive away. So do lots of people—Vancouver now supports two car-sharing services, and dozens of North American cities now offer similar setups. But Flechas and Castillo score extra points for effort; when they make tracks for the nearest vehicle, they schlep three bulky, oversized car seats along with them.

As I chatted with this model green couple in their spotless apartment—it apparently takes only fifteen minutes to clean—I kept coming back to the absence of traditional consumer goods. What stuff they do have is meticulously curated, rich in meaning, and durable. A small tribal mask on the wall reminds them of a trip they once took to Bali. A small set of dishes on top of the kitchen cabinets was a wedding gift from Castillo's mother. As for the bent-plywood Eames chair cradling my rear end, well, let's just say it didn't come from Costco.

Further, there were no toys in sight, a realization that filled me with hope. In our media soaked Western consumer culture, most playthings are not the wooden trucks and cloth dolls that fire the imagination of youth. They are not the durable objects, rich in developmental value, that we all imagine our children enjoying.

They are forged in China with gaudy injection-molded plastic, bathed in lead paint, encased in all-but-impenetrable packages designed to resemble television sets, and forklifted by the millions into bulk-shipping containers, where they make their way to suburban Big Box parent traps across Canada and the United States. The toys—essentially licensing vehicles derived from moronic animated TV programs that we parents park our children in front of to distract them just long enough to make dinner—typically flash lights and drive around on little rubber wheels, running into walls and emitting insufferable loud squawking noises. The FedEx guy brings them three times a year—at Christmas and on birthdays—and within a matter of months, they are either broken or ignored. Eventually, the battery-operated plastic machines end up in a landfill, where they will remain, in some form, forever.

Like many families, we deploy the kiddie cable channel as a tool of last resort. It focuses attention when we need it focused. (A deadline at work, a tricky recipe on the stove, an overseas call on the line.) But it also drives our children's appetites for awful products that Elle and I do not want in our home.

Although Flechas and Castillo have a television, they do not have satellite or cable. Instead, they use the TV to screen carefully chosen children's DVDs they borrow from the library. Their kids also tune in to the urban life channel, which airs 24/7 on the floor-to-ceiling picture right before their eyes.

"Our little boy—he is really a boy, and we have two fire stations out here," said Castillo, gesturing down and out the windows. "He knows all the trucks, what they are for, what they do."

"I can't see the SkyTrain," she added, referring to Vancouver's rapid-transit system, the tracks for which are mostly underground in the downtown core, save a sliver of elevated guideway barely visible from their suite between far-off buildings. "But he knows where it is, and he knows when the next one is coming."

By banning the extended advertisements that pass for cartoons these days and that unspool around the clock on satellite and cable television, this couple has effectively removed one cog from the demand-creation machine. They are successfully advancing that tricky first *R* in the universal green mantra—reduce. When birthdays come to the Flechas-Castillo home, the FedEx guy brings only books, which are easily edited off the shelf.

This clan fits so well in such a small space because they have opted out of the consumer machine that we families often find ourselves drawn into. They don't buy a lot of stuff, so they don't need to invest in the shelving they would normally need to keep it all tidy. But don't they regret anything? Don't they ever want to escape the closeness of the city?

"People say they need some privacy," said Flechas. "They don't want to see other people, so they go to their single-family detached house. But guess what? When you go into your yard, there is your neighbor in his yard. When you go on your balcony, there he is on his balcony. Is that private?"

"What about the green spaces?" I asked, picturing my island's wild forests, crisscrossed with miles of trails that are, for most of the year, completely deserted. "Doesn't that hold some appeal?"

"Most people think that when they move out of the city, they are going to look at the trees and the ocean or the rivers," explains Flechas. "If you are commuting, then you see that ocean twice a day. Without having to commute all that way, we still have the ocean. The problem is, most people feel they need *private green*."

Indeed, this desire for private green explains why my wife and I bought as much land as we did, why we assumed as much debt—a loan that Elle services with endless bus rides and insufferable corporate visioning meetings. The private green is a powerful drive in our culture, a reaction against forced density and a corollary of the nesting instinct. A small piece of private land with a house on it is the ultimate life goal for millions, including me. As my kids grow up, they will have their own patch of rain forest to play in. They'll build tree forts out in the cedars. They can't do *that* in a park. Doesn't everyone want that? If I can pay for it, isn't my family entitled to the private green?

In response, Castillo told the story of a female friend who once lived with her husband and baby in a downtown apartment. "Wonderful woman," she said, "no makeup, wears Blundstone boots. Loves gardening."

The friend had a tiny patch of dirt in a community garden quite close to her home. In summers, she decompressed there after work and dinner while Dad watched the little one. Although the shared plot was nice, for her the pull of the private green proved overwhelming. She craved a little slice of her own backyard where she could set up the playpen and turn the soil without anyone looking over her shoulder. She worked hard; she felt she deserved her own hoes and rows. She felt her child deserved it.

"So they bought a beautiful house about four years ago on the Drive," Flechas said, referring to a leafy, left-of-center old neighborhood on the city's east side that's not too far away but, as the name suggests, not walkable from downtown, either. "Now she has that small garden that gives her a fix of green." Unfortunately, her job is in the opposite direction from the single Sky-Train station that serves the Drive. So she takes the bus, with a stop at day care. The commute takes an hour each way. "Now she realizes that, being a working mom, the time she has to work on her garden between Monday and Friday is zero."

"They have this space they can't use until the weekend," he continued. "And it is a lot of work to keep up a house."

"So they spend Saturdays and Sundays doing their cleaning and maintenance work on the house instead of working in their garden," I speculated.

"Exactly," replied Castillo. "So what has she really gained?"

Not much, I admit—but the detached-home dream isn't just about a private green. It's about a sense of entitlement that is drummed into us from childhood. It's about our own piece of the rock. But the Flechas-Castillo family has another advantage on its side: Mom and Dad are both immigrants.

"We started eight years ago with a suitcase," said Flechas. "When I arrived here, I didn't know anyone, and I had no English. The problem for people who were born here and grew up here is that there is a lot of social pressure to live a life in a certain way."

And evidently, those who didn't grow up here quickly learn how one is expected to behave.

"All the people whom we know through the immigrant community, all the people who came from Colombia after us with several kids—they are out in the 'burbs. They tell us, 'I had to get my wife a big, good safe car! Bigger than the other cars!'"

"So we talk to other immigrants about how we live downtown and they tell us, 'There is no way I am going to let my boys downtown, near all those *gangs!*'" Castillo wailed sarcastically. "'All those lesbians! All those homeless people!' Well, I work in an HIV ward, and when we walk around downtown with the kids, I say hello to some of my patients. We know some of those street youth by their first names. It is OK for my children to be part of that. It is OK for them to see that!"

This unfiltered-reality approach has its advantages, she explains.

"Every time we have trouble with the kids eating here at dinnertime," Castillo continued, "We just go downstairs and across the street to see all the homeless lining up at the church kitchen."

I imagine doing the same thing with my little Sabrina, who declines all unpackaged foods except soybeans, cheese, yogurt, and broccoli. I have not yet come across this soup-kitchen strategy in any child nutrition guidebooks, but I imagine it is highly effective. We don't have anything like it on our storybook isle. We have squatters and drifters here and there, but they generally stay out of sight.

"We grew up in a city of ten million," said Castillo. "It is OK for me to be close to a stranger. It is OK for me to be close enough that I can smell the guy beside me."

"And there are germs!" said Flechas, playacting the collective urban neurosis. "I need to be protected from those germs!"

"You know, there's a product for that!" I offered, suggesting a good aerosol blast of Febreze.

All joking aside, there *is* a product to protect your children from the unknown. It is the promised privacy of a detached suburban home and matching suv—a mobile isolation chamber where the only microbes are those rocketing out of one's own boogery nose. It is a private green, where the neighbors can't spy you frantically digging in your garden because it's Saturday and you have only two hours to relocate the compost box before the kids wake up from their afternoon naps and you have to revert once again to jigsaw puzzles and YouTube space-shuttle launches.

And as Flechas and Castillo acknowledged, the piece-of-the-rock ethos is so profoundly enshrined in our culture, so celebrated, that is almost impossible to imagine a life without it. But we all should at least try to, and these two do. It's no mean feat: To thrive on the nineteenth floor in a region of more than two million, Flechas and Castillo must necessarily unplug from many of the consumer trappings of contemporary family life. They have effectively dropped out. They have climbed aboard an architecturally and socially engineered 659-square-foot lifeboat.

Flechas called it the Game, this roaring world just outside his front door. "You have to play the Game, but we are taking things out of the Game," he said.

"Don't you find yourselves constantly negotiating your interface with the world?" I asked.

Castillo sighed deeply. "Every. Single. Week."

I imagine this negotiation in and of itself takes a decent measure of life force. Commuting is not fun, but neither is signing up for an endless series of small negotiations with your spouse and your children about what not to buy. We are all working to simplify our lives, not make them more complicated. And although their home appeared spare and attractive, it represented a continuing series of conscious actions and compromises and deliberations. As much as I loathe battery-powered plastic crap from Big Box land, life on autopilot is so much easier. Then there is the inevitability that these kids will grow up and into a society that their parents have not so carefully edited.

"Do you worry that your children are not going to be able to function in the world?" I asked. "The pressure to conform, and consume, especially when they become teenagers—it's going to be tremendous."

Castillo jumped in. "I have a plan."

"Of course you do!" I said.

"It's not going to work, but at least I have one. It's Uganda."

Castillo hopes that when the kids get older, her medical training will allow her to take a teaching rotation at Makerere University in Kampala. But this is hardly a solution, either. Removing pieces from the game is perfectly fair, but in my book, dropping out of consumer society entirely isn't.

But there was already a hint of trouble on the horizon, a flicker of rebellion in this model eco-family. "Our three-year-old loves our apartment," allowed Castillo. "She invites her friends from day care over to jump on our bed. But in her mind, she knows there is something else out there. She starts telling stories to her dolls. And the stories are about a big house. With a basement. And a rec room."

It seems the couple's quiet preschooler secretly dreams of suburbia.

* * *

In my house, the private green is sacrosanct. Officially, it is what Elle and I have worked toward for ages. Thanks to our years of hard work and careful planning (and a handful of dot-com era stock options), our defense amounts to the same garden-variety entitlement that any Blundstone boot aficionado might claim. We could summarize it thus: "The kids will have their goddamn tree forts and ride their goddamn bikes in the goddamn lightly trafficked road and chase squirrels and set up lemonade stands on the sidewalk, and they will walk home from school without tripping over any goddamn junkies or finding needles on the lawn and that's *final*."

"I have lived in big cities for years," says Elle, who didn't *exactly* utter the rant quoted above over dinner the day I visited the Flechas-Castillo home, but who has, over the years, served time in New York, Orange County, San Francisco, Albuquerque, Hamburg, and Berlin. She did say this, though: "I don't want the city anymore. I hate it."

And that was, effectively, the somewhat frosty end of that. But quietly, in my head, I still admit these green pioneers have me wondering. Downtown life would be almost palatable for me, if we could afford to do it with just a little more elbow room, if we could somehow escape the preprogrammed craving for private green, and if the urban landscape were a little more family friendly. Castillo is right: I don't have time to build a tree fort anyway—I'm working too much to pay for my right to do so. If we could make downtown living work, Elle would certainly get more time with our kids—the one aspect of our present scenario that she struggles with the most. If only there were some way to find our tribe down there in the skyscrapers, some way to avoid the dirty looks from the young and single and Prada'd on one hand and the knowing-but-relieved glances from the empty nesters on the other.

Then I heard about Village 22, a business concept and branded community model that David Gottfried, one of the founding fathers of the modern-day sustainable building movement, is now shopping around the investment community in the United States.

"The problem with high-rise culture today is that the people who live there, well, they don't like kids," says Gottfried, who spearheaded both the U.S. Green Building Council and the World Green Building Council. He now runs a consulting business and lives in Oakland, California, with his wife and children, aged two and seven. "The middle-class model is the home in the suburbs, and no one who is middle class or upper middle class is living in a downtown high-rise. They are empty nesters or single or young couples."

A quick glance at the pages of condo ads in Vancouver's newspaper confirms this. The young professionals in them appear to be *precisely* twenty-nine: Just old enough to afford a down payment but not quite ready to spring for the full *Baby Einstein* library. "The suburbs are good for families," Gottfried continues. "There are kids everywhere, you get the bake sales, the soccer fields. We need all that, but we need it in the urban context, where we can walk everywhere. We need shared nannies, we need a good playground, and we need to socialize with people like us."

That's why Gottfried cooked up Village 22, so named because it is designed to bypass the twenty-first century's chronic housing problems and move right on to a better era. It's a new downtown community concept specifically engineered for families of all stripes—an ultra-green, urban mixed-use development, adaptable to various cities and circumstances. It offers precisely the kind of happy chaos that, with the exception of the odd asphalt playground, is missing in our urban cores. And it's designed to be both sustainable and affordable.

"Residents would share a green-life family concierge," explains Gottfried. "A wellness center might offer Pilates and yoga. There'd be on-site community day care, a playground, and small private offices. You could live there and play there and work there."

It sounds a bit like the Flechas-Castillo setup with friendlier neighbors, a tad more elbow room, and perhaps a little less militant anticonsumerism. Would it work for my almost-green family? No. I don't think we're prepared to give up our friends. We have already forged close ties with our community, and we're just not prepared to uproot ourselves. Our long-term answer is to somehow move our work closer to home, instead of the other way around.

Such a scheme isn't out of the question. We're fairly resourceful people, and by hook or crook we'll find a way to hang on to our private green, which, at least for now, is a little more private than most. Yes, the commute is heinous, but the flip side is a strong and authentic sense of community and history, funky shops and great schools within walking distance of our house, pebble beaches, forests of towering cedar, fir, hemlock, and maple, open spaces and open doors. In the summer, every weekend feels like a getaway right here at home, and that's got to save us a few pounds of CO_2, right? My point is, these things all have value attached that cannot be plugged into a spreadsheet. The commute is truly dreadful, but whenever we do the math in our heads, we still feel the slog is worth it. For now.

But what if there were no option like mine in the equation? What if it were early 2003 and we rented downtown and my wife were pregnant for the second time? What if our single and childless city friends were fading into the background, as they tend to do in such circumstances? What if we were being pushed by demographics and economics to choose between detached-home suburb A, B, or C? Each would, of course, be served by a carefully sited Starbucks or Home Depot or Toys "R" Us or Wal-Mart; each would perhaps be organized around a bogus town square, straight off the drafting table. Each would offer a number of suitably generic neighborhood developments with intentionally winding streets and focus-grouped names that smack of contrived authenticity, like Meadowlands or Yew Gardens or Round Hill.

Given those options, I think I'd sign up for Village 22 faster than you could say "compact mixed-use development." Would others? The father of the modern-day green-building movement is, at this moment, finding out. As I write this, Gottfried is PowerPointing the concept around a string of high-level development companies across the United States. Demand for green anything is finally surging; Gottfried's credentials are triple platinum. Who knows—perhaps the idea might see the light of day.

Just before getting off the phone, Gottfried leaves me with a little gem. "Vancouver is one of my suggested test markets," he allows.

I resolve to not mention this over dinner.

5

The Last Straw

I f the nouveau-green movement has an official shape, it is the circle. Picture the universal recycling logo of three curving arrows in a tight, endless loop portraying the movement of raw materials from cradle to cradle. You'll find something similar on a poster explaining composting, the hydrologic cycle, or the carbon cycle. Our spherical planet as seen from space is both an enduring icon of our collective fragility and a hopeless eco-cliché. Ditto our dear old friend the sun, joyous source of all life and happiness on Earth.

A circle also quite nicely charted the progress of my Eco-Shed project as of mid-February 2007. In my quest to build an environmentally sensitive writing studio, I'd found myself trapped on a kind of green-building carousel going around and around. Designers, contractors, researchers, and consultants have at various points hopped aboard, tossing me opinions and truths and tidbits of insight about materials, location, costs, and mechanical systems, before leaping off with a wave and, occasionally, some of my money. All have assured me that the journey is the destination, that the brave new world of sustainable building is simply not a process that can be rushed. Once the homework is done, they promise, the actual construction part will go very quickly. Swear to God.

But the ride was starting to make me queasy. The Eco-Shed wasn't some trust-fund, blank-check, weekend-warrior home-improvement lark. Nor was it a reality television show, in which Elle and I move into a nice hotel for two weeks, remove our blindfolds on cue, and find our dream-green studio all finished and nicely landscaped and floodlit. It was messier than that, and we wouldn't have had it any other way. We have a knack for biting off more than we can chew. And we were in a phase of life when things were generally trickier to navigate, which is why we were constantly exhausted and sniping at one another. If ever there were a time for a path of least resistance, this was it.

The pressure was ratcheting up, because the more time I spent on the studio, the less time I spent hustling up work. I had limited—and expensive—child care, and in spending my day care days researching green-building strategies, I wasn't holding up my end of the household balance sheet. I could no longer afford to noodle around with charrettes and visioning meetings. My green-building agenda was in danger of going south, along with my confidence that I could even get the damn thing built at all.

Meanwhile, there was still a rust-streaked foundation slab in my front yard, attached to the back side of my father-in-law–financed double carport. It was now the middle of February, my wife was making polite inquiries on the status of the project, and I had nothing to tell her. There were no lines of orange spray paint in the front yard; no little wooden pegs flapped with surveyor's tape. To borrow the technical language of the building trades, I had fuck-all.

* * *

I thought I had it all figured out two months before. After weeks of gentle lobbying, Heather Choi, my twenty-five-year-old designer and green-building researcher, had convinced me that the Eco-Shed should be a straw-bale building. She made a compelling case: bale buildings offer excellent fire resistance, great pest resistance, and, critically, impressively high insulation values. Straw is relatively cheap, easy to obtain, endlessly renewable, and reasonably straightforward to build with—you bolt together a timber frame, stack the bales inside it, then slap on a coat of plaster. Plus, there are already two homes here on my island made out of the stuff. There was one serious catch with the program, though—a fundamental shortcoming that nagged away at me. But when Choi and I got together on one particularly dreary winter day in early December, we weren't yet debating the pros and cons of dried grass. We were talking about the schedule.

Choi and I were at a ritzy West Vancouver latte joint, the sort of place where they have comfy leather club chairs, Italian mosaic tile, and a special sign explaining how rarefied their espresso machine is. We were about to meet with a renowned green-building designer and consultant, a man who has over decades designed dozens of beautiful, durable straw-bale homes in Canada and the United States. We'd hoped to retain him to review and critique Choi's still-forthcoming construction drawings. But in the lead-up to his arrival, I told Choi that I was anxious to move things along, that we were already beginning to drift off the schedule we'd established together.

"I hope you are not frustrated with the process," Choi said as I took a deep draft on my latte. "But the nature of the way these things have to work is they are very heavy on the front end and then quick on the back end. That might sound counterintuitive."

"No, it sounds completely intuitive," I replied. "You want to get everything figured out, you want to get it just right."

Of course, I was lying. I was deeply frustrated with the process she was referring to. With so-called integrated design we'd identify efficiencies, reduce waste, and end up with fewer costly change orders and delays later in the process.

We'd held one of these design meetings a month or so earlier. Hardly anybody showed up; most of the invitees were all too busy on far more lucrative projects. Nonetheless, I was happy to make the effort, so long as Choi was actually putting pen to paper in the background.

"You have been doodling and sketching, all the way through this process, right?"

"I have been sketching since we began," Choi assured me, "and researching West Coast modern architecture. I am gathering all this for a design meeting, but it's a good idea to know what we are dealing with before we go out and say, 'The building will look like this.'"

Although this was all true, I reiterated that things still appeared to be moving too slowly for my liking. It was early December, we'd been working together for several months, and after all this researching and investigation and fact finding, I'd still not seen so much as a sketch on the back of an envelope.

Meanwhile—though of course it had nothing to do with Choi's foot-dragging ... er, diligent investigations—I was spending money far faster than I was making it. Try as I might, I couldn't seem to score the kinds of assignments that I badly needed, i.e., lucrative gigs that didn't require travel (see also: primary caregiver). And so Elle and I took the first of many nibbles on the Eco-Shed's credit line. She logged on to our account and made the first of many transfers to cover our groceries, swimming lessons, and the like. It was a terrifying moment, the proverbial thin edge of the wedge, the first line of a Coen Brothers movie starring us, a transfer that bankers have seen a hundred times and share with one another over a beer after a round of golf. My grand sustainability experiment was already proving to be nothing of the kind, and the realization made me cranky. I needed to get the project underway as soon as possible, get it completed soon after, and move on to the thornier issue of aligning my career with my domestic reality.

There was a lot at stake. You know the story: foreclosure, bitter divorce, custody battle, alcoholism, cirrhosis, etc., etc. It wasn't supposed to happen this way. The Eco-Shed construction timeline Choi and I had drawn up together suggested that an early spring completion was plausible. But without blueprints, I couldn't hire a contractor, let alone get a meeting with one. They were all otherwise engaged, building custom three-thousand-square-foot McMansions on the back side of my island, surfing the hottest real estate market in Western Canadian history.

Without drawings of my humble little shed, I couldn't get a bid, I couldn't get a commitment, I could barely get a call back—let alone a building permit. Given the current pace of the project, I imagined obtaining a set of blueprints some time around March, only to find no one available to help me build them out until the end of the summer.

Foreclosure! Divorce! Custody battle! Etc.!

Choi tried to talk me down off the ledge. "We have done a lot of work on this project," she said, reassuringly. "All of our players are almost in line, and all this research, all this knowledge we are accruing right now—it's all information that, in a normal design process, would be happening in the later stages of the game. Once we have enough info, then we can make really informed decisions about what we are doing."

I took a deep breath and closed my eyes. *Calm blue ocean. Calm blue ocean. Calm blue ocean.*

"I would really urge you to relax and enjoy the process and have some faith that this is going to come together quickly. You are thinking in very small particulars. Things will come together."

Exactly one month after this conversation, without having had the anticipated design meeting—indeed, without supplying so much as a pencil sketch on graph paper—Heather Choi unplugged from my planet-friendly Home Office of Tomorrow.

"It has become apparent to me, for several unforeseen reasons, that I am no longer the best person to take your project further," she wrote in an e-mail.

My green-building carousel of despair had just picked up speed.

* * *

In the epic saga of the Eco-Shed, Choi's resignation was, as they say, a low moment. But remember, whenever a door closes, another one swings open. And though I'm not the sort of guy who typically buys into such Up-with-People claptrap, that's almost exactly how I came to work with Dan Parke. In the most delicious irony yet for a project that is in part about the power of thinking locally, it turned out that the perfect architect for my project lives and works, as the crow flies, fewer than 250 yards from my house.

A contractor friend had suggested I try Parke in early September. I'd spoken with him back then just long enough to ascertain that he was already overextended and couldn't possibly take on any new projects. Besides, by that point I was already underway with Choi. What a difference a few months can make. While I was off on my six-month merry-go-round, Parke was moving a number of contracts off his desk. Fortuitously, just as my eco-goth and I parted company, he was starting to come out of the weeds. After a few weeks of judicious courtship—at one point, I left a six-pack of microbrewed beer on his doorstop—he agreed to take me on.

Having Parke onboard filled me with hope. As it turns out, we shared much more than a neighborhood. Like me, he knows too much; he has a rich understanding of the mess we've all gotten ourselves into, but similarly, he struggles to fully embrace sustainability in his own life. He, too, is accredited by the Canada Green Building Council, and he's helping to shape an ambitious sustainable development planned for the west side of the island. But like me, his own spec home won't win any green-design awards. We both have small families, we both regularly overextend ourselves, and we're both blessed with patient and supportive wives waiting in the wings to help pick up the pieces when we crash and burn. And twice a week, we both find our inner peace not through sun salutations and warrior poses, but by kicking the crap out of a series of leather sparring bags at our island's Tae Kwon Do studio.

Shortly after parting ways with Choi, I'd vetoed the straw-bale route. Although the two straw buildings already on Bowen were holding up well—both were built in the early years of this century—I decided that the material presented too much of a risk for my liking. The culprit? Rain. Straw must be kept dry at all costs. As any farmer will tell you, once a bale gets damp, it begins to rot. And although contemporary straw-bale buildings are designed to be shielded from damp—from below by elevated foundations, from above with generous roof overhangs, and from the sides by layers of breathable plaster—I am not fully convinced that the scheme was a fit for a spot where it can easily sluice down for thirty consecutive days and nights and where a good deal of that *agua* blows sideways all night long at freeway speeds.

Neither is my federal government. In 2000, the agency responsible for building research released a lengthy technical report on the impact of moisture in straw-bale buildings. The study noted that straw-bale walls in wet coastal climates experience higher moisture content. But the jury was still out on whether this constant damp would eventually rot them into the ground: "It is not yet clear whether this will lead to a significant wall failure rate."

In other words, the unequivocal scientific answer to the question of whether soggy, windswept Bowen Island might be a suitable spot for an Eco-Shed built with compacted livestock bedding was as follows: "Uh, beats us." And although straw may indeed work fine with the proper details in place, I'll leave it to others to finish the experiment. I'm brave, but not *that* brave.

For his part, Parke didn't want anything to do with the stuff. "You can't put in any safeguard," he said. "You put up the bales and you plaster both sides and that's fine. But as soon as you get any cracking—and you *will* get cracking; all plaster will crack—you have potential for moisture getting in there."

I'd witnessed cracking plaster on my faux adobe home back in Santa Fe and the moisture part on Bowen, having just emerged from one of the most brutal winters in the island's history. Wind drilled January rain against the side of our house like a trigger wand at the carwash. "Once that moisture's in there," said Parke, "you're hooped."

There were other drawbacks as well. The home insurance industry is not wild about straw, and although grass grows pretty much everywhere, you need extremely tight bales to make a house. The nearest supplier of so-called building bales was more than a thousand miles away. In other words, there was nothing local about it.

So, if we weren't going to build with straw, I deduced, perhaps we should use mud. For the better part of a year, that's what custom furniture designer Burns Jennings had been trying to tell me. After more than a decade spent as a carpenter on the island, building houses with traditional framing lumber, insulation, siding, roofing, and so on, like me, Jennings came to realize that the way we build our homes has to change. "I remember the day really clearly," he told me over beers one day last summer.

"I was framing up a house and I said to myself, 'In about thirty years' time, this whole thing is going to be rotting back into the forest.' I mean, that's what wood does. Unless you treat it with toxic chemicals, it's an organic, biodegradable product. Why are we even using it? Why don't we build our homes to last for generations instead of just a few decades?"

Jennings was planning a new home for his own wife and two young sons, and he knew there must be a better way to do it. He just had to find it. So he hit the books, spending

God-only-knows how many hours researching green-building strategies. He investigated straw, concrete, and everything in between and finally landed on a method of building energy-efficient, mold-and-pest-proof, earthquake-resistant homes out of a stabilized, insulated, rammed earth, a material and a system developed in recent years on Salt Spring Island, some forty miles to the southwest of us, just north of the U.S. border.

With traditional rammed earth—the kind that has been used around America and the world for centuries—builders construct a wooden form, then fill it with layers of damp soil, which they individually tamp and compact with posts or hydraulic rams. After the earth has dried, the workers pull off the forms, leaving the finished wall. Unfortunately, this traditional version of rammed earth offers poor insulation and uncertain earthquake performance. By contrast, the technique's latest iteration uses stabilizing cement, reinforcing rebar, and rigid-foam insulation. The finished wall is gorgeous, glassy smooth, and all but impervious to the elements. It is, in a word, indestructible. The rammed-earth Jennings home might well prove to be the Stonehenge of Howe Sound. Far from melting into the forest after a few decades, it is expected to endure for centuries. And best of all, my new best friend Dan Parke designed it for him. Perhaps Parke could cook up something similar, on a much smaller scale, for my front yard?

That's how I came to be running numbers with my new black-belt green architect. As Parke and I tinkered with the spreadsheet and attempted to pound the realities of rammed earth into my budget, those numbers didn't look so good.

"Let me shoot from the hip here," said Parke. "My preference is to do a rammed-earth building on your site. But it is an expensive type of building. The cost of materials is really high, the labor is really high, and on Bowen Island, labor is in short supply. The good people are all really, really busy. Even the mediocre people are busy. So ideally, you get really good people, but ultimately, you get who you can get."

"So, what are we talking about here?"

"OK, rammed earth is going cost 15 to 20 percent more than traditional two-by-six construction. But from a green point of view, I am always saying, try to think longer term. Think maintenance and operating costs."

"Right, I know, I know," I said. This was the official motto of my carousel ride, and by this point I had it memorized. Consider life-cycle costs. I'll save on energy, and my electricity bill will be lower. With rammed earth, I won't have to repaint my siding five years from now—because there won't even *be* any siding. "But I still need to come up with the additional money to build this way upfront."

Parke shrugged. "I have been through this number crunching before with other people, looking into rammed earth versus stick frame. And they can't rationalize it either. They are in the same boat as you. They have X number of dollars to work with, period, and even if, over twenty years, they will be spending fewer dollars on operation and maintenance costs, they still need to finance it right now."

"That is the central conundrum of green building," I said.

"It's one of the big ones," he agreed. "Banking is not set up to deal with it; it doesn't take into account long-term life-cycle costs. Nothing does."

Back to the spreadsheet. After factoring in the so-called soft costs, which include Parke's fee, engineering, permits, surveys, and so on, and dividing the money remaining by the planned size of the Eco-Shed, we ended up at $171 a square foot. It wasn't enough, said Parke. Given all the variables, a stabilized rammed-earth building would need to run closer to $200 per.

"Something is going to have to give here," said Parke. "If you still want to pursue rammed earth, your budget will need to be higher or the square footage is going to have to come down. But you can shave down the size of your space to a point where it doesn't make sense to build it."

We tried that approach anyway. Trouble is, the scale of rammed earth is massive. The walls are two feet thick, and construction costs are calculated from a building's outside dimensions. Reducing the overall footprint to bring down the square footage squeezed out the living space, too. My Eco-Shed was on its way to becoming an Eco Closet, a classic case of diminishing returns.

"What if I did just one rammed-earth wall, maybe the north wall?" I asked, remembering we would need a thermal mass in the building. "Could we tie a stick-frame building into a rammed wall?"

Parke had already asked this of Meror Krayenhoff, the entrepreneur who had developed the most promising stabilized and insulated rammed-earth system to date. "You get seismic issues," Parke said. "A rammed-earth wall is going to behave very differently from a wood-frame wall. You want it all consistent on the same floor. If you want to do wood frame on a level above the rammed floor, that you can do."

"OK, let's forget it," I said. "It's out-there enough already to use rammed earth as a building technique. To push the envelope and make it into some kind of unproven structural hybrid—that seems too risky."

"So where does that leave us?" Parke asked.

I agonized.

"To hell with it," I declared. "I am going to have to get more money." I would poach it from Elle's landscaping budget. Perhaps she wouldn't notice?

"Good for you," said Parke. "I hear you on the money, though. I tend to do smaller, more interesting projects, and that means I don't get paid at the corporate rate. If I were designing shopping centers, I could afford to build my own studio."

"We suffer for our art, don't we?"

"Indeed we do."

We took the overall budget up another fifteen thousand dollars, and after deducting the soft costs, ended up with a writing studio around 250 to 300 square feet. I went home and poured myself a Scotch. I made it a double, in honor of my budget, which has all but done likewise since I first conceived this cockamamie plan. "To stabilized insulated rammed earth!" I said, toasting nobody in particular but already feeling the hangover of near-certain financial ruin that I'd just signed up for. The payments on the new place would cripple me. I mean, Jesus, Mary, and Joseph, why couldn't I just lease a hybrid like everyone else and leave it at that?

Indeed, why couldn't I? The idea was certainly tempting. The slab was still sitting out there in the yard; ditto my grim carport. A Prius might have been expensive, but the unofficial icon of the carbon-reduced life was a screaming bargain when lined up on the balance sheet alongside my one-man crusade to reinvent suburbia. What if common sense had seized me then? What would my life be like today had I put down my single-malt at that moment and called the whole thing off?

Things would probably be easier, quieter, simpler. I'd doubtless have funneled our money and eco-ambition the same place most keen greens do: the soil. Our still-on-the-sketchpad victory garden would bloom into a lush respite of fruit trees, berry bushes, veggies, and herbs. We'd have a few beehives up in the woods, maybe a mead-making operation in the basement? A few hens out back would feed eggs into the Glave family protein supply chain. Heck, maybe we'd get a goat, which would eat our compost and just about anything else not nailed down in exchange for milk. Lot 55 would be an Edible Eden, a cul-de-sac homestead. After a hard day working the crops, we'd lounge in the garden, reading magazines and plucking grapes dangling from the arbor, our backs to the carport and rust-streaked sarcophagus. The kids would be hooting and hollering on the rope swing I'd set up for them out in the forest, the rope swing *I'd actually have time* to set up for them. Indeed, I imagine I'd have lots of things: A surfeit of leisure. More hair on my head, because I wouldn't be pulling my hands back over my scalp as I tend to do when the pressure bites hard. Actual leisure weekends, whiled away as they were intended: on restorative, marriage-recharging family enterprises such as scouring the shores of Deep Bay for beach glass, or skipping stones out at Killarney Lake …

I snapped back to reality. *Beach glass?* Screw that! I'd come this far, I wasn't about to pull the plug on my schemes yet. Seeking support for what was increasingly becoming a highly leveraged operation, I ran the rammed-earth idea by the wife. I opened up the glossy coffee-table design book a friend had sent over and showed Elle pictures of a gorgeous rammed-earth home in Arizona. You could see the faint lines between the courses of material in the massive walls, an effect that evoked the soothing organic pattern left by waves on a sandy beach. Of course the bastards had shot the place at sunset; desert twilight danced off the home's rich burnt-umber surfaces. It was magical. And it could be ours.

"Oh my God, this place is amazing," Elle gushed. Then she caught herself. "Isn't it super-expensive, though?"

"Well, yeah, kind of," I admitted. I didn't share all the gory details from my meeting with Parke. "We couldn't build it on the pad, though—the walls would be too thick. We could do it next to the carport. It might take up a bit of our garden space …"

This was a devious move, because she didn't yet know that I intended to cost-shift our planned fruit trees and spend the money on mud, cement, and rebar.

"Well, OK, if you think it has to go there, then I guess I can live with it," she replied. My wife wasn't about to convert our future garden space into a parking ramp, but a rammed-earth studio that glowed in the winter sun like a Mexican mission? Evidently, it wasn't entirely out of the question. It would look mighty strange alongside our carport, but perhaps some landscaping would soften the transition?

I e-mailed Arno Schmidt, the Vancouver-based rammed-earth contactor who would lead the mud-mashing crew at the Jennings place, an eco-palace that I imagined would be the toast of Bowen Island and possibly the world. Schmidt and I had had lunch in Vancouver a few months back, just before Choi talked me into straw bales. I asked him what it was about my project that appealed to him. "You're basically doing an experiment," he'd said, tucking into a Reuben sandwich. "That is about leadership. So I said to myself, 'Here is somebody who wants to lead instead of follow,' and that is my vision as well."

He had showed up for my understaffed charrette, had a look at my slab, and offered numerous suggestions, but like Parke, he didn't do straw. It was time to bring him up to date. "I would love to reconnect with you about the idea of doing my writing studio in rammed earth," I wrote in my e-mail, "perhaps ganging up the project with the Jennings job if the timing makes sense. What do you think? Could we pull it off?"

Yes, we could pull it off, he replied. But then, when we connected on the phone a few days later, he asked a more difficult question: Why would you want to?

"I've been thinking about your project," Schmidt said. "I know you're interested in energy conservation and following a path that leads to a smaller footprint. And I asked myself, is there any way you could somehow still use this semifinished pad foundation you have there? Wouldn't it be more advantageous to ask yourself, 'How can I get what it is I am after without following the path I have told myself I need to follow?'"

On my end of the phone, I silently channeled Edvard Munch. I'd finally convinced myself that the slab, lacking any southern exposure, would simply not work for a passive-solar Eco-Shed. After several thousand revolutions on my green-building merry-go-round, I'd assured myself that the best course of action was tearing the concrete out and starting from scratch. Embodied energy be damned! Now Schmidt was sending me back to square one.

Foreclosure, bitter divorce, custody battle, etc.

All I could muster was a feeble, "Huh?"

"I don't want to push you in any direction," he continued, "but one of the things I realized a long time ago is that I really need to speak my truths. And I've come to realize that you could spend less money, and use fewer labor and material resources, to accomplish the same goal. Maybe it's not what you have come to imagine, but you can throw money at stuff and that doesn't mean you are making a difference."

He was right. How could I possibly inspire others to leave a smaller footprint if doing so meant tearing out a few tons of concrete foundation and pouring a new one twenty feet to the east, representing more emissions, more embodied energy,

more materials? More, more, more! How could getting deeper
into debt mean anything other than extra commuting, longer
hours? I racked my brains. There had to be another way to
build a passive-solar shed on the 280-square-foot concrete slab
that I already had, with plumbing and all the rest already in
place.

There was. And it took a black belt of green architecture to
show it to me.

6

Culdesactivism

Each night before climbing into bed, I went through the same routine. I shut down the laptop, killed the TV, fired up the dishwasher, checked the doors, and switched off the lights. I peeked in on the children, then headed to the bathroom and reached for my toothbrush.

Then, as I scrubbed a lifetime's worth of crowns and fillings and my precious few remaining lumps of intact enamel, I would idly wander over to the bedroom window and spend the next two minutes staring at my neighbor's floodlights.

Five of them were mounted across the front of his house, and although I had not inspected them up close, each likely contained a sixty-five-watt incandescent bulb. I knew the fixtures were controlled manually by a wall switch, as opposed to some dusk-and-dawn-sensor, because some evenings they remained dark. But many nights of the year, they were on, illuminating the front of my neighbor's home for no particular reason that I could discern.

Security is certainly not yet an issue here on Bowen Island. Crime is minimal, and on my street, there's no shortage of nosy neighbors—including two police officers—who note the comings and goings of those who belong and those who don't. We also share a moat three miles wide. The last ferry pulls away from the island's dock at 10 p.m. each evening, marooning any would-be visiting catburglar until morning.

As we have by now established, I am a mildly obsessive man, and the five floodlights just over yonder ranked high on my list of concerns. On those days when the end of the world just wouldn't go away, I would lie in the silent blackness thinking about what the lamps represent. On the plus side, here on Canada's West Coast, the electricity is not as thick with hidden greenhouse gases as it is in many other parts of North America; a scant 10 percent of our juice contains CO_2. But those five beacons across the way were still doing atmospheric damage. I had already done the math on what we might delicately call my neighbor's nocturnal emissions, and as best as I could calculate, the lamps were kicking up something in the range of ninety-five pounds of carbon dioxide a year.

In the grand scheme of things, that's atmospheric chump change. It is the equivalent of about three return trips to Grandma's house in my SUV, and I easily find ways to justify those excursions. Hell, I probably endanger more polar bears just by vacuuming the house and doing my laundry, which amasses around my house in great fuzzy piles like tribbles on the starship *Enterprise.*

It was unfair of me to pick on my neighbor, whom I shall call David. But there was something about his all-night Light Show for Nobody that I couldn't quite keep my mouth shut about. In my head, his lamps had come to symbolize all the little things we all could be doing to save ourselves from extinction if we only knew better. They are one of thousands of minuscule course corrections we would each make if we had the right information and the right kind of encouraging nudge, delivered at the right time in the right way. If each of us took all the baby steps to overcome unconscious bad habits we didn't even know we had, we could dial back the planetary thermostat. We could unleash staggeringly good changes.

That hasn't happened yet. We haven't welcomed that helpful nudge, because for so long, it has felt more like an obnoxious push. For the longest time, well-meaning environmental advocates have been selling us the wrong message. The world is full of really big problems, they've endlessly instructed, and it's your job to buckle down and help fix them. As American political strategists Michael Shellenberger and Ted Nordhaus wrote in "The Death of Environmentalism," a pivotal discussion paper published on the Web in 2004, "Most people wake up in the morning trying to reduce what they have to worry about. Environmentalists wake up trying to increase it."

To force us to wake up and make changes, the enviros used the best tactic they could come up with: guilt. It failed spectacularly. For years the public response to their chronic alarm raising has been to quickly change the channel. Life is stressful enough already. Jesus, look at the time! We haven't even done the dishes yet, and I have to be on an overseas conference call at 7:30 a.m. Did you make that pediatrician appointment today like I asked you to? And hey, isn't *America's Next Top Model* on at eight?

Happily, the greens have begun to recognize this wild disconnect. By talking about solutions, not problems, by pointing out money to be saved or made, not spent, the greens have turned public opinion around. Environmentalism's radical image makeover hasn't hurt, either. Who wants to be green when the role models are living in trees and shitting in plastic buckets?

Fortunately, the tide is finally beginning to turn. The campaigns that are starting to see results—the ones that people are beginning to connect with—are all about the easy, attainable things that can have a real effect. They stress the simple solutions that are staring us in the face.

Which is why I couldn't stop thinking about those floodlights. They were the proverbial low-hanging fruit, rendered in glass, tungsten, copper, and aluminum. My neighbor could have made a small but not insignificant difference by simply not turning them on. Just by embracing darkness, he could have made a difference. Both of us would have felt better—well, OK, *I* would have, at least until I found some other hapless SOB to blame for our looming mass extinction. And for those nights when he still felt the need for a little illumination, he could have pulled out a stepladder and replaced the bulbs with compact fluorescent versions, which would slash the juice for the same job to a slow trickle.

The trouble is, there was no easy way for me to communicate either option to David without putting him on the defensive. If I approached him about his lights, the first thing he'd doubtless do would be to rightfully point to the vehicle sitting in my carport, which leaked many times more pounds of carbon each year than the fixtures mounted on his cedar siding.

Yes, the SUV. I was working on that. But in the meantime, knowing I was no emissions angel, how could I break the ice with David without crippling our healthy, over-the-hedge relationship?

* * *

For advice, I turned to Solitaire Townsend, the cofounder of Futerra, a consulting firm in London, England, and a leading authority on the tricky business of talking about global warming in a way that inspires action, not antipathy. Townsend recently coauthored a fascinating pair of documents chockablock with strategic advice about climate-change communications: "The Rules of the Game," commissioned for the government of the United Kingdom and released in 2005, and "New Rules, New Game," released the following year, which speaks to a wider audience. Both papers are evidence based: they explain what works and what doesn't, based on dozens of academic studies of consumer behavior-modification campaigns. They're rooted in lessons learned, rather than assumptions made, about how we might talk to one another about this stuff.

My hunch that a casual driveway chitchat might turn ugly, as it turned out, was bang on. Rule 18 of "New Rules, New Game" flags the "sod-off" factor, which researchers more properly call psychological reactance: "This means that many people's automatic reaction to 'You must do this' is a simple 'No!'"

Meanwhile, another pointer cautions, "Don't criticize home or family."

Clearly, I had my work cut out for me. So how could I motivate David to turn off his floodlights once and for all? To save the world, it seemed, I needed to start thinking more strategically. I needed to operate more like a PR guy. I needed an engagement strategy.

I sketched out my quandary to Townsend, who cooked up a game plan for me on the spot. "One of the first things to realize is that the things that have motivated you to act may not be the same things that have motivated him," she counseled. "One of the big problems of this movement is that it assumes everyone reacts in the same ways. Unfortunately, and wonderfully, people are motivated by different things."

What prompted me to start doing something about global warming was my preschool-age offspring. But the first bullet point in Futurra's first study is "Don't rely on concern about children's future." Indeed, my neighbor and his wife have no kids.

"The first thing to ask yourself is, 'Why does he have the floodlights?'" continued Townsend, a former actor who went on to complete a graduate degree in sustainable development. "It could be that he likes seeing what is outside. To understand where people are coming from, their reasoning has to be understood. He may be emotionally attached to the floodlights."

That was certainly not out of the realm of possibility. I am emotionally attached to a source of twenty-four-hour electrical illumination—one that Elle and I had installed in our living room wall. We own an instrument called a Geochron, a wall-mounted rectangular box about the size of a large atlas opened up flat. It reveals, in real time on a slowly scrolling world map, where the sun is shining on the Earth. The Geochron is a cool gadget, nothing more—a wedding present from an old friend. It runs on a small electric motor and a pair of slender fluorescent tubes.

At night, the Geochron casts a faint blue glow across the main floor of my home. Its light spills out my windows, such that my neighbor can see it from his place in what is otherwise my pitch-black house. Like his floodlights, perhaps, it serves no useful purpose other than decoration. Unfortunately, the damn thing is not nearly so easy to switch off. To do so, I need to partially pull it out of the wall, a delicate operation. If it were as simple as hitting a button, I would simply power it down each night on my way upstairs like everything else.

"The second thing to know," continued Townsend, "is 'Thou shalt not' or 'Thou should not' is the wrong way to do it. So is, 'I am perfect.'"

Given my aforementioned attachment to artificial light, not to mention my suv, I was indeed far from faultless. And if there's one thing I can't stand, it's an eco-pariah. But knowing what I do about the mess we've gotten ourselves into, knowledge has become a lonely burden. Each of us is at a different point on the road to green, and sometimes I find myself biting my tongue in the name of keeping everything copacetic. It's not easy. I'm choosing my battles every day: What do I keep my mouth shut about, and what do I try to gently tweak?

But the lights, *the lights* ... I just couldn't let them go. I had to somehow inspire my neighbor David to kill them without tripping his "sod-off" response. Really, I have to get everybody's floodlights off, without turning into the kind of meddling, pushy jerk I would doubtless quickly revert to should Elle suddenly pack her bags and make a break for Albuquerque. This immediate goal, the one right in front of me—let's call it Operation Dark House—required a delicate touch. I threw myself on Townsend's mercy.

"The best situation you could have is that he chooses to get rid of the lights without you having ever said anything about it," she counseled. It seems I needed to sell David on the benefits of blackness, even while I cast useless light into my own living room and balcony all night long. I needed him to think that we're all in this together, that we're each doing the best we can. If I played it right, I'd start to see those bulbs burning less and less when I wandered over to the bedroom window at night. If all went well, he'd think it was his idea.

As a journalist, I find this notion a little uncomfortable. I've dedicated my career to countering spin and questioning advertising, to exposing manipulative and persuasive language. Now I was supposed to embrace it?

Townsend was sympathetic, to a degree.

"If we genuinely and truly believe what is happening with the climate is, in fact, happening—if we are convinced of that—then we have to pick up the tools of marketing and communication that have been used exceptionally well to sell us a huge set of behaviors for a long time."

"A lot of people are very coy about picking up these tools. Because, yes, they are manipulative. They feel that if we just educate the public enough, then people will change. It doesn't work like that."

My mind cast back to that "Death of Environmentalism" essay and its assertion that classic save-the-whales enviros squandered unimaginable amounts of time and money by treating us like eager young students, by presenting images of destruction in an effort to shame us into action. They should have been listening to Madison Avenue.

"It may feel strange to you," Townsend continued, "but if it takes a bit of social engineering to have a conversation with your neighbor about changing his lights, then that's what it takes."

"It feels more than strange," I replied. "It feels disingenuous. But I suppose at least it's disingenuous for the right reasons."

"One of the issues we face is that most of the people who are very good at influencing other people's decisions have gone into marketing," she said. "So either we pry them out of there and make them come over to our side, or we are going to have to suck it up and learn how to do it ourselves. We are not always going to be in our comfort zones with this stuff."

No kidding. I've always been impressed by people who really know how to sell—a skill I equate with postadolescent trauma. While still in my teens, I took a minimum-wage mall job flogging cheap and trendy fashions to club kids and other self-conscious poseurs. It lasted less than a month. After I'd occupied the bottom spot on the register-tape sales ranking for one too many days, Joanne the boss lady fired me. "I'm very disappointed, James," she told me, smiling sweetly. Really, she did me a favor. Joanne showed me, at the dawn of my professional life, that I lack the social graces needed to move product. Evidently, I scared away the customers. Can you imagine?

But now, a lifetime later, I found myself heading back to that metaphorical sales floor. To get David's lights off, I was going to fashion myself into a leader of sorts, a new kind of suburban activist—one armed with the latest global-warming sales-and-marketing tactics. I was not going to use images of pending doom; I was just going to make darkness seem sexy and desirable, just as Cameron Diaz has done for hybrids. And, by taking a page from "New Rules, New Game," I was not going to do it alone. I was going to use what Townsend's paper calls a change group.

"The hardest thing you are going to do is change just him," she said. "Invite a few neighbors over and decide to do things as a group. Find a way not to be the dominant force in the discussion. Have somebody else lead it, so it will feel less like it is being forced on him. And if you can, hold your tongue when they decide to do a few things that you know maybe aren't so good or useful. You should applaud those ideas all the same."

By this point, my neighbor—who has been reading over your shoulder—is either tittering nervously or simmering in a slow-build rage. With luck, I have not once again mangled a personal relationship. And David, if I have, I hope you will some day find it in your heart to forgive me for making an example of you. When the power goes out again this coming winter, help yourself to my firewood stash.

But I digress. "What if I worked the money-saving angle?" I offered. "What if I installed a compact fluorescent bulb in my own porch light and raved on about my savings?" This is precisely how many green-savvy companies, including Home Depot and Wal-Mart, are carefully and tentatively advancing a sustainable agenda. There's nothing about greenhouse gas emissions on my curlicue-light packaging. But there is a little blurb about how much money the bulbs could save. Is this the best route?

"The power bill can be a really helpful gambit," offered Townsend. "But the trouble with economic signals is that they can change. For example, power may get cheaper." That makes sense: take away the reason for the change—saving money—and you might take away the change.

We returned to the idea of peer pressure and having somebody other than me playing emcee.

"Food helps," said Townsend. "Having food and alcohol at a meeting such as that really helps. And biting your tongue. If you offer a really nice evening, maybe trying a whole load of local foods, and they have eaten your food and drunk your wine, then—and *only* then—do you introduce the idea of changing habits as a group. You could approach it as a challenge to the next town over. But however you approach it, wait until they have eaten your food and drunk your wine. Then they'll feel beholden to you."

"This is starting to sound like a press junket," I said, feeling queasy, "or worse, a time-share presentation."

"Don't hit them up for what you want until they have already been wined and dined," she stressed. "If you try to talk to them first—if you try to use the meal as a reward for action—they will only do the minimum that they feel the food is worth."

So a few days later, I e-mailed around an invitation to a potluck dinner. I asked guests to bring something local to eat or drink and invited them to rent *An Inconvenient Truth* beforehand. Then I added the following:

We would like to host an after-dinner discussion the same evening on the theme of how we can as neighbors reduce our greenhouse gas emissions, even in small ways. Perhaps we can share rides to the city when we need to go there, or even just a lift to the preschool one day a week. Perhaps we can commit to walking to the village or picking up things for each other. We all have different situations and challenges—some of us commute regularly, others schlep kids all over the place—I hope by putting our heads together, we can come up with a few ways to cut a little more carbon dioxide out of our daily lives.

I closed the message with a few stats on where most of our town's emissions come from (cars). I did not mention vanity-driven exterior lighting.

When people find themselves in a socially awkward situation, they often react with humor. Sure enough, the RSVPs were full of comic relief. "I'd be glad to pick your kids up in the new Hummer we just got," responded Marty, our compulsively sarcastic veterinarian friend. "Bright yellow. Like a school bus. Perfect."

Marty cc'd the whole invite list, and others ran with the ball. "We're taking the kids kayaking to hunt for the last albino baby seal," replied John, an actor friend who lives down the street. (The seals again!)

Then the next-door neighbor who unwittingly inspired all these shenanigans in the first place chimed in: "We've been having problems with predators at our salmon farm, so we're scheduled to join the sea-lion hunt that day. The good news is that if we can make it back in time, we'd love to join you and will make sure to bring some fresh meat."

The change group was already working its magic.

∗ ∗ ∗

I wanted to serve a local dinner. Of course, late January is about the worst time to try such a stunt. But Townsend had told me to make my neighbors comfortable, show them a good time. So I trucked down to the butcher at my local Whole Foods and asked for some organic beef that was as regional as possible, within reason.

I'm not very good at buying flesh unless it's destined for the grill. Ribeyes and chicken breasts? I'm your man. But when it comes to shopping for a big slab of something for the oven, I am invariably suckered into buying too much of a cut I can't afford—a scheme that never fails to land me in hot water—or something unworkable at the other extreme. For the same reason, I do not send my wife out to purchase lag screws or drywall. We each have our areas of expertise. Entertaining and meat procurement are her department. But the reality is, she has a desk job, and I'm usually the one buying the groceries. So, fresh from the pediatrician, with three-year-old Duncan pulling at my arm, I appealed to the butcher for help.

"All of our beef comes from an open-range ranch in British Columbia," she said, offering me a pamphlet with a picture of what looked like an honest-to-God cowboy on the front. The steer pictured inside looked happy enough; a few dozen of them browsed in a grassy field.

"I'd like to do a roast for about eight people. What are my options?"

"The prime rib is our best cut, lots of marble in the meat," she replied. "That would be very tender, really nice."

"How much?"

"Eight people?" She did the math. "You're looking at about eighty-five dollars."

I like my neighbors, but not that much. "What are my other options?"

There were three other rows of string-trussed bovine to the left of the overpriced flesh she had just returned to the case, in descending order from prime to subprime to way below prime to something that resembled a knot of organic, free-range gristle. I had other middle-course options but somehow ended up closer to the far left, in the chuck. Literally. "Chuck roast is a leaner cut," the clerk explained, offering full disclosure, "but it'll be very nice if you cook it for a long time at a low heat."

Sounds easy enough. And at twenty-six dollars, I could afford to buy it, with enough left over for hundred-mile-compliant carrots.

"Keep a lid on it, keep it moist," she instructed, as she handed it over. "You'll do well with that."

Everything in the Whole Foods vegetable section was from California, so I dialed Capers, a natural-foods market a couple miles down the street that I knew specialized in local produce. "We've got Jerusalem artichokes and celery root," the produce manager offered. "Not too much else from around here at this time of year. Everything is sort of finished."

I had no idea what to do with either. "I'll be right over," I said.

Saturday rolled around. Accounts vary on what happened next, but I could've sworn the butcher instructed me to cook the beef for four or five hours at 275 degrees. Dinner was at seven. Allowing time to rest on the counter while the geographically desirable vegetables finished up, I carefully installed my precious planet-friendly roast on the oven's middle rack early in the afternoon. I placed it under a tent of foil with some water in the pan. A couple of hours later, as delicious aromas filled the kitchen, it was time to check on the meat's progress toward perfection. I extracted the evening's piece de resistance, pulled back the foil, and stuck my friend chuck with a meat thermometer.

Hope turned to dread as the red needle instantly zoomed past "beef-rare," "beef-medium," and "beef-well." Like a runaway box car, the thermometer's pointer only picked up speed from there. It moved onto other animals, rocketing right through "lamb" and barely pausing at "poultry." Finally, the gauge ran out of livestock options altogether and, after pulling a double-jointed full rotation, came to rest off the scale, in an unmarked zone that should properly be labeled tanned goods.

In panic, I reached for my mobile and dialed Beef 911. Elle answered, and after listening to me describe the symptoms, pronounced the roast dead over the phone. "It's lunch meat," she said, clearly disgusted with me. "Go get something else and start over."

I loaded Duncan back into the SUV and drove to my island's gourmet butcher shop. There I shelled out sixty dollars for a prime rib roast from Alberta, for eight people, proving once again that when it comes to sustainable consumption, you can always do it almost right the second time—usually for only slightly more than what it would've cost you from the beginning.

From there, the meal went together fairly well, for the most part. Although the local carrots, celery root, potatoes, and onions all roasted up wonderfully—alongside the not-so-local prime rib—the knobby Jerusalem artichokes bordered on the bizarre. The only workable recipe I could find required peeling them— an immensely tedious and dangerous task that Elle cursed her way through—then layering them with sliced ginger in a gratin. It was awful.

Nobody seemed to mind. Five couples showed, and everyone got into the spirit. Someone brought a plate of local cheeses; another, a blackberry pie that began its life in a thicket of canes growing alongside one of the island's nicer beaches. Elle made an apple crumble with the flavorful fruit the kids and I picked last fall in Feenie's Orchard, a tucked-away nearby grove of gnarled century-old trees. We quaffed Gulf Islands pinot gris and a fantastic meritage from the Okanagan Valley, British Columbia's answer to Sonoma. Organic chocolates rounded out the picture, crafted by an artisan operation on Bowen called Cocoa West Chocolatier, less than a mile from my kitchen.

With everyone suitably sated, I kicked off the discussion by introducing a special guest. Fellow islander Paul Welsh runs a public-relations firm and helped launch the City of Vancouver's climate change public-engagement program. Directly inspired by the "Death of Environmentalism" essay, the OneDay campaign (onedayvancouver.ca) is about small moves to change your routine for the better—such as cycling to work, if that is realistic—for just one day out of the week, or even one day out of the month. It stresses the easy stuff: Turn off that idling car, dial down the thermostat a degree or two, adjust the pressure in your tires. And, critically, turn off unnecessary lights.

"The OneDay program builds off one of the key tenets of social marketing theory," said Welsh. "And that is, if you can make a behavioral 'ask' of people that is easy, obtainable, and simple in its beginning, you can build momentum and make the 'ask' bigger a bit at a time. Make it small from the start, make it easy, and get emboldened by success early. Then you can ask for more."

OneDay is a clever, broad-ranging program. It employs the tools of viral marketing—plus sophisticated branding and a fully realized visual identity—to help communicate its breezy, let's-roll-up-our-sleeves message. Best of all, like Wikipedia, the whole thing is open source. Anyone in any city or district anywhere in the world can download, for free, a OneDay start-up package that contains everything needed to localize the scheme and roll it out in his or her town. The legwork has all been done; Welsh and others have engineered OneDay for self-replication. It is a virus of change looking for receptive hosts.

And it finds one in my living room. "Imagine OneDayBowen," suggested Welsh. "You want to tap it tomorrow? Go ahead. Download the tool kit; use our posters, our logos, our brochures, our decals for your car windows. It's all right there on the Web site."

Preprimed as they were with delicious food and wine, my guests were all over the idea. I'd invited Paul over hoping our friends and neighbors might like to not only turn off superfluous lights like the ones inside my Geochron but also sample a few more of the program's baby steps ("wash laundry in cold water"). But within the space of an hour, the assembled would-be-greens went much further. It was as if I'd opened a faucet of pent-up forward motion. Shackled perhaps by the thorny social dynamics of the greener life, everyone had been looking at each other, waiting for someone to say, "Go." Someone just did, and that someone was me. At the urging of Jen, a contract business consultant, my guests committed on the spot to launching the whole program here as OneDayBowen. Another attendee—Stuart, who works in the shipping industry—went ahead and registered the domain name the very next day.

I handed each departing couple a swirly light bulb on the way out the door, and after the last guest had put on his coat and left, Elle and I started cleaning up in pleased silence. In the space of a few hours, what began as a contrived and manipulative plot to push my neighbor to switch off a few floodlights turned into the seeds of a grassroots movement. Townsend had warned me I'd be operating outside my comfort zone. She was right, but for the wrong reasons. It wasn't that I felt like a slick marketing exec that evening. Paul Welsh had played that role quite capably—hey, it's what he does for a living. But I was still in psychological terra incognito. After a career spent looking on from the sidelines as a wise-cracking skeptic, safe as a neutral and "objective" journalist answering to nobody except my editor, I found myself drawn toward something else. Something unfamiliar, but also invigorating: grassroots community activism.

That night, as I brushed my teeth at the window, I looked out across the yard. The lights were dark.

7

Indomitable Spirit

"Why don't you just take this down?" Dan Parke asked, waving at the carport in all its asphalt-shingled glory as we stood in my front yard one day in February. "This is blocking your sun. Get it out of here."

A switch clicked in my head. Heather Choi and I had already covered this ground a few thousand revolutions back, endlessly shuffling around spaces and pieces, but I wasn't emotionally prepared to face the family fallout I imagined this decision would unleash. After all, my father in law had paid a small fortune to build the structure for us as a housewarming gift just two years earlier.

But on that February day, I realized I'd turned a corner. At some point in the preceding months, I had emotionally divorced myself from Padre's shelter, along with the grande-sized vehicle inside it that we were working up the nerve to sell. It was easier to let go of the structure once we had a sense of what would replace it, and here Parke had proven his weight in microbrewed beer. He'd sketched up an Eco-Shed so blindingly cool that it easily eclipsed all the unsightly asphalt and concrete that came before.

The Eco-Shed would be one of the greenest, most energy-efficient buildings on my island. For reasons of budget, we would build it with wood, and for reasons of embodied energy, we would use most of the concrete foundation slab we already had. We'd take back our sunshine by deconstructing the carport—reusing and recycling as much of its carcass as possible. The new building would be a classic passive-solar design. In the winter, when our great ball of fire swings low through the southern sky, skirting the top of a nearby ridge, its rays would pass through a wall of glass and warm the exposed concrete floor within like a giant pizza stone. That heat would have no place to go, thanks to reams of foam insulation we'd install in the studio's floor, walls, and ceiling. A small, efficient electric boiler would help things stay cozy on miserable sun-free days by circulating warm water through loops of plastic pipes laid in the slab. And when the power blipped out—as it does rather frequently on Bowen Island in winter—a small, high-efficiency woodstove would step into the breach.

In the summer, when the sun tracked high overhead, generous roof overhangs—the southern portion would extend six feet out from the wall—would shade the studio and its occupants from the heat. And that epic ocean view to the east that Helen Goodland counseled me to consider very carefully? It'd still be there, framed on the wall like a piece of valuable artwork, visible through a window just two feet high by five feet wide.

The Eco-Shed would be heated by the sun when it was available and flooded with natural light. It would offer its occupants excellent indoor air quality and humidity control with help from a heat-recovery ventilator—a piece of mechanical equipment designed to exchange stale, humid inside air with deep lungfuls of fresh outside sea breezes without sacrificing much precious heat. The space would incorporate high-efficiency plumbing fixtures and lighting and as much reclaimed material as possible. Its oversized long-life steel roof would harvest rainwater and fill a 2,400-gallon cistern that would in turn irrigate the organic fruit-and-vegetable garden planned for the surrounding yard. Native grasses would sway in the breeze out front where a spread of polished concrete once lay.

All this time, the solution was right there in front of us. The place would be green, without leading us too deeply into the red. And with the weeks ticking down to my late-spring deadline, it was time to get cracking.

Literally.

* * *

Tom Roocroft clung to the cab of his Volvo EC210 excavator while I settled into the ergonomic seat within. The longtime contractor had agreed to let me take the first swing at Padre's lightly used timber bunker—and all the vehicle-centric thinking it represented—using the sole source of his livelihood: his $300,000 machine. "The controls are very pressure sensitive," Roocroft explained in an easy and familiar manner that suggested he offered rides like this all the time. "The faster you move them, the more quickly the machine responds. So try to go easy on 'em until you get a feel for what they can do."

Of course, I already knew what they could do. This is a modern-day T-Rex, engineered to dig deep holes, demolish concrete buildings, and juggle monoliths of bedrock. It's probably overkill for this job, but I needed Roocroft's mechanical muscle because I also wanted to restack the ugly heap of boulders alongside the property line that I share with my neighbor just to the west. By rebuilding this retaining wall—at the moment a haphazard jumble of very large rocks—hard up against the boundary, I'd be able to maximize my new parking space—a short lane that would eventually be paved with recycled bricks or some other permeable surface. With the car tucked off to the side, I'd remarkably improve the view from my Eco-Shed's large south-facing windows. Instead of staring into the front grill of a golden-pearl SUV, I'd see a small patio, perhaps an apple tree, and a split-cedar fence beyond.

The retaining wall boulders are too big for a mere backhoe. They require a class of machine that heavy-equipment aficionados call a 200, a machine like Roocroft's. And considering what this beast can do, its controls were disarmingly easy to figure out. I had a fighter-jet-style joystick in each hand, each one topped with a few thumb buttons. Manipulating the sticks moved the boom in and out, closed and opened the two-cubic-yard bucket, and rotated the entire machine left or right on its undercarriage. Roocroft didn't mention the two large pedals on the floor at my feet; I gathered they activated the EC210's caterpillar tracks. If engaged, this rumbling juggernaut would quite happily grind forward straight through the south wall of my home, into the mudroom, where my son, Duncan, was standing, transfixed, at the glass door.

I'd only been at the controls for a moment, but that was enough for my little guy to mentally promote me on the spot from the rank of ordinary father to that of full-fledged deity. You see, while our Big Boy is a born people person who loves a good cuddle with his mum, he is also rather fond of his machines. In recent months he has asked me to explain and sketch ad nauseum the capabilities and inner workings of semitrailer trucks, tugboats, locomotives, rockets, cranes, submarines, asphalt rollers, tanks, helicopters, blimps, backhoes, hovercraft, chainsaws, ambulances, navy frigates, jumbo jets, police vehicles, and, yes, excavators. By his specification, my kitchen-table technical renderings must include all relevant buttons, levers, throttles, joysticks, hydraulic pistons, fittings, chokes, gauges, air horns, valves, warning lights, and remote-sensing instruments. Indeed, since Elle began paying the mortgage, I have rendered all of these contraptions and more to the best of my abilities on construction paper with a washable Crayola marker. Getting your dad to draw an excavator is wicked cool. Watching him actually *operate* one? There are no words.

Anyway, I kept my feet the hell away from those pedals.

After I spent a minute or so practicing with the joysticks, Roocroft gave me the go-ahead. "Try pulling that corner off," he suggested, indicating the nearest of a series of squat eight-inch-square concrete pillars that protruded from the pad's edges. Each post once anchored one of the carport's four handsome

Douglas-fir timber legs, which, a few days ago, I'd carefully removed and set aside for reuse.

I lined up the enormous steel bucket behind the target, then worked the sticks to gingerly draw it forward. After the slightest shudder and a sound like grinding molars, the post popped off like a pencil eraser. Easy enough, I thought. Maybe I'll try lifting up a corner of the parking pad.

I repositioned the EC210's business end, gingerly pulled back on the stick, and tucked the claw underneath the edge of the pad. This time, I felt considerably more resistance. The whole front half of the parking pad very gradually lifted up, but so did the EC210.

"Maybe we should hold off on that for now, so we don't break the machine," Roocroft said calmly. Earlier, he'd pointed out a steel pin at the end of his machine's boom—essentially the axle that the bucket pivots on. It would need replacing soon, he'd said—a scheduled service interval. The job would run five thousand dollars. "I don't want to add that to your bill."

A few minutes later, I stood on the small rock bluff overlooking what was once my carport and watched the master expunge Lot 55's remaining suburban infrastructure. Roocroft clipped off a piece of concrete about the size of a small upright piano, lifted it into the air, then dropped it onto the center of the pad. Like a spoon tapping a hard-boiled egg, cracks radiated from the point of impact. Roocroft worked his improvised battering ram to pulverize a small section of the pad, then dug in his steel canines. Piece by piece, he broke up the pad and loaded it into a dump truck, which carted it away to be used as construction fill elsewhere on the island.

Although it's undeniably fun to play real-life Tonka for a few minutes, waste is nothing to celebrate, especially when the waste is concrete. That's because the stuff is made with Portland cement, the production of which generates tremendous quantities of greenhouse gas. As we shall learn shortly, cement is arguably the most emissions-intensive building material in the world; every ton of the stuff produced also produces about a ton of carbon dioxide. According to the U.S. Department of Energy, in 2005 the American cement industry released nearly 90 million metric tons of CO_2 into the atmosphere. (For comparison, every car and SUV driven in California the previous year collectively coughed out 137 million metric tons of the same heat-trapping bad news.)

The slab needed to go, but the embodied energy in that dump truck tore at me. And although the rubble wasn't going far, alas, I couldn't say the same for some of the rest of the carport debris.

I was able to save all the long, heavy fir timbers, five engineered roof trusses, and a dozen two-by-six studs. The trusses and timbers and the fasteners that locked them together would find a new home here on the island. The dozen or so two-by-six studs would vanish into the walls of my Eco-Shed. The aluminum storm gutters went into Bowen's light-gauge metal recycling bin. But the rest of it—1.5 tons of plywood sheathing, roofing paper, asphalt shingles, and assorted bits of painted trim and nail-studded two-by-fours—ended up in a landfill about 160 miles away.

I wanted to reuse and recycle those materials. Really, I did. But in attempting to salvage them, I learned two things. First, our modern-built environment is not easily disassembled—thanks largely to the labor-saving invention of the nail gun, a pneumatic tool that vastly speeds up suburban carport erection. Time really is money to a builder, and the nail gun radically accelerates the framing process. But it also makes firing twenty-five nails into a stud as easy as firing six. Whoever built this suv shelter in 2005 had the tool's pressure set too high, not to mention a very eager trigger finger. Not only did the dude absolutely pepper the framing with extra grippy spiral-shank fasteners, he sank the heads of many just below the surface, making them almost impossible to remove. Just for fun, I conducted a random audit: One standard two-by-six stud contained sixty-three nails. I extracted every single one from that board and a dozen others like it, and my right rotator cuff still feels the strain. Similarly, I'd hoped to reuse much of the plywood sheathing on the roof. It came off in splinters.

The second lesson of my deconstruction exercise proved even more disheartening. In *Cradle to Cradle*, starchitect William McDonough advances the idea that "waste is food." Picture the kitchen scraps that make their way to the composter, then as soil back into the garden, which helps nourish the next generation of vegetables. It's the same thing with steel and drywall. If you put in enough thought and effort, McDonough argues, many of a building's constituent parts can usually be reclaimed or recycled in a way that can save—or even make—the developer money. And indeed, I was able to sell the carport timbers and trusses. But in other areas of the Eco-Shed project, waste sadly turned out to be just that.

The carport hosted about five hundred square feet of lightly used asphalt roofing shingles. When the time came to take them down, I imagined myself loading them into a friend's trailer and diligently pulling them to a recycling center like so many neatly tied bundles of newspaper. There I imagined they would be ground up and used to resurface roads or runways. Waste is food, right?

Well, maybe one day.

After eight or nine phone calls—half of them to the Recycling Council of British Columbia, a terrific organization that did its best to connect me with an end market for my roofing—I discovered that used shingles (known in the trade as "tear-off") can't go into street asphalt, because they are contaminated with other materials, like sand and felt—not to mention nails—and road surfacing is mixed to precise engineering specifications. It turns out that much of the tear-off diverted from landfills is pulverized and burned to make ... cement. I called up Randy Gue, a director of resource recovery for Lafarge North America, to get a better handle on the process.

"When you make cement, you take raw materials—silica, gypsum, limestone—and you mix them and burn them in a kiln," he explains. The materials are transformed at very high temperatures into a hard material called clinker, which is in turn pounded into a powder. The CO_2 comes not only from the burning of fuel to fire the kilns, but also from calcification, the chemical process that drives the gas out of the limestone along the way. "The typical fuel of a cement plant is coal, and we look for alternatives to coal," says Gue. And if a series of planned trial runs with tear-off proves successful, and if regulatory approval arrives as planned, discarded asphalt roofing might be one of those alternatives. Gue was hoping to burn the stuff in his Vancouver-area cement kilns within a matter of weeks. Some of it could be mine.

Then again, both tar and coal release copious amounts of greenhouse gases when burned. In 2005, the two coal-fired cement plants on the southern outskirts of Vancouver—LaFarge owns one of them—together spirited the equivalent of about two million metric tons of CO_2 up their stacks and into the atmosphere. For comparison, in the same year, all the cars in the region collectively contributed 4.3 million metric tons. The cement industry is experimenting with wood waste as a coal substitute, and good for them, because wood is more or less carbon neutral. But that doesn't help me with my shingle problem. Do I really want to unleash all the CO_2 sequestered in my unwanted roofing?

Next I tried Sean Mabberley, owner of Urban WoodWaste Recyclers, an innovative company that processes some 180,000 tons of construction waste in Vancouver and nearby communities. An impressive 45 percent of that total is recycled—metals are culled for smelting, and wood scrap is processed into biofuel. Mabberley told me that he normally only works with big industrial operations but that he'd grind up my shingles into cement fuel if I brought them over, unloaded them, and paid him eighty-five dollars per ton for the pleasure. But I had to ask him, isn't a landfill a better final resting place for my shingles than the atmosphere?

"There are not so many good options," admits Mabberley. "You have two choices for fuel: you either dig it out of the ground, burn it, and send up a bunch of emissions, or you use something that you are going to have to throw away anyway and burn it. Then at least you are not digging up the ground."

Logically, that made sense, but then I factored in the effort to get my roofing to Mabberley. Round trip, it's a thirty-seven-mile drive to his facility, plus the costs to "recycle" the shingles, plus the twenty-three-dollar ferry fare. Then there was the time: it would cost me almost a full day. All this just to burn a small pile of tar in a kiln and hurry along the gradual grim torching of our lush planet. It wasn't exactly the kind of reincarnation I had in mind.

As I pitched my shingles into a large yellow bin that would cart them to a landfill—part of the 1.4 million metric tons of tear-off that the industry says is discarded each year in this country— I flashed to the moral message at the end of *WarGames*, the 1983 Cold War classic starring a teenage Matthew Broderick. After running more than a hundred global thermonuclear war simulations—all of which end badly for everyone—the film's supercomputer character concludes that "the only winning move is not to play." Asphalt shingles may be the cheapest roofing option on the market today, but they may be the most expensive in the long run. My home is covered in thousands of them.

So is every other place in the neighborhood. And in about two decades, they will need to come off.

* * *

Roocroft eradicated the carport slab from Lot 55 in the time it takes to skim the sports pages. Then he moved on to smash another crucial section of concrete—the one in the middle of my rust-streaked sarcophagus. Like the carport, it, too, represented embodied energy. But there was no way to use it in the Eco-Shed because our original builder had neglected to place any insulation beneath it. Without this styrofoam stratum, each winter evening as my island rolled away from the sun at a leisurely seven hundred miles an hour, whatever precious free heat we'd captured within would leak into the bedrock below. But with a credit card and a little help from Roocroft, I was about to start nudging that warmth in the other direction and keep it in the building.

At least I didn't have to wreck the whole thing. Our contractor had formed the studio slab in two separate stages. First he poured a continuous six-inch-wide perimeter footing. Picture a large, straight-sided rectangular concrete bathtub, and you get the idea. He routed the plumbing pipes and electrical conduit into their proper places in the midst of this "tub," then filled it with compacted sand to within four inches of the rim. After laying down a layer of plastic sheeting, he frosted it flush to the perimeter with concrete. Presto: sarcophagus.

My new and improved plan called for four inches of wall-to-wall rigid foam insulation on top of the sand. At that thickness, the foam has an insulation value four times the standard. Anxious to get a jump on the construction, I asked for this so-called R20 foam at the island's building center.

I was met with puzzled looks. "R20? I don't think they make it," said Pat Buchanan, a wonderful and warm man who sports Jesus hair and a bushy mustache. Buchanan has worked at the Bowen Building Centre for decades and also helps take care of Endswell Farm, which at forty acres is our island's single largest agricultural operation. Clearly, he doesn't get much call for R20 foam. "The rigid stuff is rated R5 for half an inch," he explained. "If you wanted to go to R20, that would be four inches thick. You could always sandwich a couple of two-inch pieces together." Although I strive to support local businesses, I ended up placing an order with an off-island supplier. Cost: $1,084.22. By that point, I'd spent just shy of $20,000 on the project.

But unless I wanted to make a Superbowl-scale beer cooler, I couldn't yet legally do anything with that thousand-dollar foam when the truck deposited it on Lot 55. Everything I had done so far—the sawing, the shingle pulling, the digger driving—could be loosely classified as site preparation. But the moment I glued a sheet of pink foam to the inner edge of my foundation, I crossed a threshold. I was technically—at long last—actually *building* something. And for that, I needed a building permit.

Which is how I found myself wandering up and down my street one Sunday afternoon in April, knocking on doors, a freshly minted set of Dan Parke's marvelous Eco-Shed plans rolled up under my arm, my two adoring children holding each hand like a couple of politician's props. I was pounding the pavement and kissing babies in search of buy-in.

I had my supply list nailed down, my "critical path" largely dialed in. Or so I thought. But one last obstacle stood in the way of my subversive green-building agenda: a one-page memo, buried deep in the mountain of paperwork attached to the title of my property. In 1999, when this hillside was still second-growth bush laced with logging trails, a clutch of planners and architects drafted a set of look-and-feel rules properly called Section 219 Covenant for Design Guidelines. The regs were intended to "secure a commitment to quality and a strong overall character that will add value to the community, maintain the value of each purchaser's investment and ensure an uncompromised level of livability."

Livability. Quality. Return on investment. It sounds like Section 219 was lifted directly from the green-building song book, but unfortunately good intentions don't always play out as planned. Although the de facto style rules have succeeded in creating a consistent neighborhood aesthetic—we live in a kind of seaside-cottage Disneyland—they don't exactly support the future-proof principles of passive-solar architecture.

"The adoption of a theme, such as the West Coast rendition of original Cape Cod design or Arts and Crafts features may serve to complement existing island styles and add to a sense of community," the guidelines explain, before sketching a few specifics. "Facade design may include articulated rooflines ... accessory buildings must be similar to the architectural design, material and color of the house ..."

This may be an appropriate time to mention that the Eco-Shed, my proposed accessory building, does not neatly embrace an Arts and Crafts or West Coast Cape Cod theme; nor is its roofline articulated; nor is it in any respect similar to the architectural design, material, and color of the house. In fact, it doesn't resemble my pad in the slightest, and for a very good reason. Although there will be backup heating systems inside the Eco-Shed, namely a small woodstove and a hydronic radiant heat system, my preferred source of wintertime warmth will be our Heavenly Great Ball of Fire. Contrived heritage charm isn't driving my studio's design; performance is.

When it comes down to it, the faux Arts and Crafts bungalows in my 'hood are all about the past. They are designed to visually echo the area's historical early-twentieth-century vacationer cottages, some of which are gradually rotting into the ground in the village below us. The new homes were intended to be affordable for young families like mine. They meet and do not exceed the requirements of the building code, they largely ignore the sun, and they are mostly warmed with energy-hogging electric baseboard heaters. These simple and inexpensive devices—they're basically wall-mounted toasters without bread slots—help lower the sticker price on a home. But like asphalt shingles, they cost more in the long run; they suck juice like a frantic preschooler. My family and those living in the homes around me have probably already erased the initial "savings" the appliances offered via regular payments to the power utility—payments that, in a saner world, could have financed what it would have cost to do it right the first time.

From my earliest sit-downs with Helen Goodland and Heather Choi, "Section 219 Covenant for Design Guidelines" had loomed large on my list of concerns. To me, it had come to symbolize our damaging attachment to the past. The guidelines are a testament to the profound power that the idea of heritage still holds over our culture. You can build an Arts and Crafts bungalow out of sustainably harvested lumber, you can dial back on its toxic finishes and insulate and ventilate the place like crazy, but so long as it ignores the sun—which it probably would do— in my mind the building won't be "green." In slavishly supporting an early-twentieth-century motif, one established long before the age of climate modeling, the home style of my neighborhood (including my own place) is only compounding our troubles.

I'm going to get voted off the island for saying this, but I've concluded that history now belongs in the hands of preservationists, not architects and developers. Thanks largely to inertia, James Kunstler's psychology of previous investment, and the comforting emotional familiarity of the past, heritage-style homes built today will not serve us well in the coming decades. Shake-trimmed dormer windows may be authentic in a J. Crew catalog kind of way, these designs may offer a reassuring sense of continuity, but the stakes in this game have gotten too high for us to ignore what we now know. If we don't start letting go of the past, we won't have much of a future. Our kids won't be sitting on the porch swing, sipping lemonade and talking about the good old days. Instead, they'll be grappling with our legacy. This doesn't mean we need to scrap centuries of style—let's not rev up the EC210s and plow under the old neighborhoods. But in making something new, performance should dictate aesthetics, not the other way around. Let's face it, the Victorians had different priorities.

I'd once asked Stacy Beamer about my design covenant. A contractor who used to design freeway overpasses but who now crafts iron sculptures and beautiful natural-stone garden hardscapes, Beamer would help prepare the Eco-Shed site for building. "Don't worry about it," said Beamer, a longtime islander who has seen it all. "Every house in this neighborhood has already broken those guidelines six times over." He was right, and my own place was a prime example. The tenth bullet point on the list states that "garages should not visually dominate the house." (Until Tom Roocroft came along the previous week, mine did just that.) That said, no house would break this contrived residential mold as resoundingly as the Eco-Shed would. It wouldn't resemble my residence in any respect, and thank God for that.

But back to the short history of my 'hood. As the millennium turned over and the cul-de-sacs crept ever higher up the hillside, the design guidelines remained largely fallow, because the man appointed to enforce them—a developer named Wolfgang Duntz—designed, built, and sold all the homes himself. In his defense, the places shared a common architectural motif, but there was nothing cookie cutter about them. They were carefully sited to maximize both the view and privacy, and when seen from the approaching ferry, they did indeed blend into the hillside. The plan worked. At least, until the market caught up with the vision.

By the time I backed a U-Haul into Lot 55's front yard in mid-2005, Duntz was in a pickle: he'd positioned the development as a small-scale, accessibly priced project for young families, but young families like mine could no longer afford them. The real estate market in nearby Vancouver had gone haywire, and Bowen felt the lift. At the same time, buyers wanted more flexibility; they wanted to buy Duntz's lots and build on them with their own crews instead of using the official team.

Duntz sold off the remaining few lots on our block to a variety of homeowners and builders; a number of them were less interested in neighborhood character and more concerned with good-old-fashioned return on investment. One or two built monster homes right up to the setbacks—neo-McMansions that made the charming Arts and Crafts cottages just down the road look like dressed-up tool sheds. While out of kilter with the rest of the block, these new homes technically conformed to the plan, because the covenant did not specify any limitations on size.

But that wasn't good enough for some. In fall 2006—just as Heather Choi and I were debating the finer points of straw-bale building—a quietly outraged representative of my neighborhood fired off an e-mail to Bowen Island Municipality, asking why it was not enforcing the design guidelines covenant. In response, the municipality said it would henceforth require Duntz's signature on construction drawings before it issued a building permit in the development. All of a sudden, another gatekeeper stepped into my critical path. The once-fallow design guidelines now loomed as large as the nearly three-thousand-square-foot home that was rising out of the mountainside above Lot 55.

"As soon as someone builds something different, neighbors will take issue," said Duntz, who, though vilified by many, had made tremendous contributions to my community, donating land for churches and schools, a golf course, and a spiritual retreat. "People like to bitch, and they disagree. But it's not my job to tell people what to build or not to build. I intend to prevent major idiocies or upsetting and revolting things."

There was nothing idiotic or revolting about my Eco-Shed, but since it did technically violate the design guidelines—to wit, " ... accessory buildings must be similar to the architectural design, material, and color of the house ..."—it might ruffle feathers. And so, before he would sign off on my permit, Duntz asked me for two things: a one-page explanation of why my studio would look the way it would (easy enough) and a collection of signatures on the plan from those who might be most affected by the construction—my immediate neighbors.

This second thought struck terror in my heart. I knew my charming children would only get me so far. Most of the people living on my street were delightful and accommodating. We'd met most of them at a block party we'd hosted the previous summer in our since-expunged carport. But one property owner didn't show up for the party that day—the guy terraforming the hillside above my place. The man we shall call Nick lived out of the country most of the time. When he did show up to check on the progress of his project, he made it clear that his panoramic ocean view represented his life's work and that he intended to protect it.

Although I'd need Nick to approve the design, I knew he would only care about one aspect of my project: how much it would intrude on his line of sight.

At least we had some ground rules. Separate from the design guidelines, Duntz and company established height restrictions over most of the properties. They protect the view of those above from those below, who might otherwise recklessly plant a leafy grove of towering bamboo. Those intending to build something in the height-restricted areas must seek the permission of those above. My neighbor David—of the now mostly dark floodlights fame—had once asked Nick if it was OK if he built a little pergola to screen his parked cars. The structure would not impact the view from above. The request was reasonable. It was flatly denied.

Of course, there was a height restriction over my front yard. And to capture every possible photon from the sun, Parke had designed the Eco-Shed's slanting roof to use almost every inch of the allowed height. So let me now frame this as delicately as my attorney will allow: My immediate neighbor to the west, Nick, was building the largest house in the neighborhood. It was arguably among the most visible on the entire island. He enthusiastically defended his property's impressive view. And he exercised his driveway-pergola veto power to a degree that others have found, shall we say, unreasonable.

Why is Nick like this? I can only speculate, but one possible explanation comes to mind: He grew up in a culture in which the rights of private-property holders reign supreme. But in a small, tight-knit island community, where everyone knows everyone— indeed, where people look out for each other as good Canadians tend to do—a relentlessly self-interested worldview does not always translate well on the ground.

I decided I'd work on improving our relationship when we actually lived next door to one another, but in the meantime, Nick quietly terrified me. A veto from him could have easily stalled the Eco-Shed for months. Although the decision to move ahead ultimately lay with Duntz, my neighbor could have theoretically dug in his heels enough to send Parke and me back to the drawing board. This delay would have been catastrophic. I had spent more than enough time at the drawing board. I felt as if my life were on the drawing board. We needed to start building. Three months ago.

My strategy was simple: I would show Nick how my little studio would improve his view and therefore increase the value of his property. First up, the memo. Although it did explain the sustainable aspects of the design as Duntz had requested, it was written for an audience of one:

The new building will present a considerably smaller footprint than the carport it replaces. At its highest point, the structure will be sixteeen centimeters below the height restriction ... It will be lower than the ridgeline of the carport it replaces ... When viewed from [above], the proposed studio represents a 26 percent overall reduction of visible roofing over the original plan approved for the site.

That was all true. Parke whipped up a few before-and-after renderings, then we e-mailed them off to Nick.

He called a day or so later, and after a few questions about the angle of the roof, he told me what I'd been longing to hear.

"So what you're saying is, you took away the carport and replaced it with something smaller, right?"

"That's right."

"So why would anyone object to this?"

"No reason," I replied without missing a beat, "except that the design of the studio does not really reflect that of the main house, and the neighborhood guidelines state that it should."

"I can't see anything wrong with this," he said. "It seems fine to me."

I tried to disguise the wave of relief washing over me. "Great. So can I mark you down as having signed off?"

Long pause. "You know, I'm coming up there on Thursday; why don't we look at the site together then?"

I ground my teeth. At this late stage, I could not afford another delay on my building permit application. "I'm kind of anxious to get moving—but yeah, we could do that. The renderings are accurate, but I understand you haven't got the full advantage of being here."

And so four days later, Nick and I stood together on my site on a Thursday afternoon in the pouring rain. He had lots of questions and was playing his cards close. He knew I wanted to get going. That just made it more fun. "How far out will the roof extend? Is it a flat roof? What will it be made of? Where will you park your car? Why did you restack the retaining wall? Is there any chance it will collapse?" And on and on.

Finally, "I don't see a problem with this at all."

"Awesome," I replied, pasting on a smile. "So all I need is your John Hancock on the plans, then. They're just inside the house here. Why don't you come in out of the rain for a few minutes?"

My neighbor didn't immediately respond or even make eye contact. Instead, he stared at my fourteen-by-twenty-foot foundation for a full ten or fifteen seconds. Then he looked up at his own project.

So did I. Over the course of a year, his work crew had spent months jackhammering and blasting and stacking boulders higher and higher up the mountainside. At one point, Nick had his beleaguered contractor assemble a scaffold in the middle of the chaos so he could climb up and survey his domain from the level of his future living room. On several occasions Nick stood up there, browbeating the weary builder, who I suspected was all the while secretly wondering how to stage a tragic accident. For weeks at a time, the construction racket had been so unbearable that we had to keep our doors and windows closed during the hottest summer ever recorded in Canada. Dynamite warning signals—a dozen staccato taps on an air horn designed to be heard hundreds of yards away—regularly rocketed Duncan from his afternoon nap. On several occasions, concrete-pumper-truck deliveries blocked the street just as we were pulling out of the driveway, late for day care again. Framing and roofing crews blasted a classic rock radio station for weeks on end. *Sweet home Alabama, Lord I'm coming home to you ...*

Yet all through this chaos, not once did Nick stop in to seek my sign-off on any of his activities. Not once did he offer so much as a hint of apology or regret for the house-rattling explosions. No phone call, no e-mail, no box of chocolates, no pack of microbrewed beer left on the doorstop. Zip. As Wolfgang Duntz put it to me in the subdued language of diplomacy, the man standing in front of me that day pretending to ignore my question was "not in a position to complain."

Nick knew this. But he also knew a few other things. First, I had no leverage: despite the ruckus, every aspect of his private Three Gorges Project was perfectly legal and legit. His vaguely craftsman-style house, though enormous, complied with the building code, the land use bylaw, and those damn neighborhood design guidelines. Second, he had more money than I did to pursue a fight if it came to that. Finally, he understood that I badly needed his signature to continue. And for reasons that only he can fully understand and probably have something to do with childhood trauma, he wasn't ready to give it to me.

"Let me think about it overnight," he said.

* * *

Each Tuesday and Thursday, Dan Parke and I begin our martial arts class the same way all the other students do—by raising our right hand and reciting the Tae Kwon Do Oath. "I shall follow my conscience," the pledge begins. "I shall have peace of mind ... I shall express my love for others ... I shall have an indomitable spirit." As my mother always told me, it's good to be idealistic. But at that moment, standing in the rain with Nick while he plainly relished the power he held over me, I found myself sipping on my last thimbleful of indomitable spirit. I was at the time a yellow belt, a mere beginner in the Korean martial art.

The secret to attaining the coveted top ranking is to live your life with what our master calls black-belt attitude. I was on my way to this higher plane, but my black-belt attitude had just evaporated.

Fortunately for Nick, that day was a Thursday. Within two hours, I would be back in my island's *dojang*—first to recite the collective oath of peace, love, and understanding, and then to kick the crap out of a handheld leather sparring bag. I smiled broadly and bade Nick good evening, after first forming a clear picture of his face in my mind.

The encounter underscores another difficult truth. When it comes to behavior change, leading environmental economists—such as my fellow Canadian Mark Jaccard—note that the stick can be as powerful as the carrot. Financial disincentives such as carbon taxes can be a powerful driver of behavior change. But not always—that four-hundred-dollar Santa Fe natural-gas bill sure did sting Elle and me, but not quite enough to nudge us into a retrofit (we later heard that the wheezing furnace imploded shortly after we sold the place). But those with the biggest footprints—the jet-setting McMansioneers who pilot cabin cruisers and collect exotic cars—well, the tricky thing is, plenty of them could give a rat's ass about carbon. The NetJets crowd have the means to utterly ignore most economic signals. For now.

Later that night, after I had released my well-suppressed rage in a healthy and productive manner, Elle congratulated me for showing as much restraint as I had earlier in the day. "If this project is doing anything for the planet, it's making you a better person," she said. "If it were me out there, I would have given him a sock in the chops."

I certainly came close, but it's a good thing I didn't let fly with a perfect Bruce Lee roundhouse. At 10:30 the following morning, after another barrage of questions ("Will there be any glare off the studio's roof?"), my kind, considerate, and very community-minded neighbor took my offered pen and inked his signature smack in the middle of my plans.

8

The Envelope, Please

To touch the giants that towered over British Columbia when the ink was still sticky on the Magna Carta, you must first head to the suburbs.

You might do as I did and hop into a Lexus RX 300 SUV, crank up the seven-speaker Nakamichi sound system, and crawl down the gridlocked four-lane highway that pipes you into Vancouver's detached-home hinterlands. You'd take the exit just before the ginormous bright blue Ikea, drive another mile or so, and hook a left at the twenty-screen multiplex. Just a little farther along, you'd pass a strip of weed-choked, potholed parking lots and rusting freight warehouses. And through the back of one of those properties beyond a couple of chain-link gates, you'd find a man sporting a goatee and a broad-rimmed leather hat who makes his living giving the past a future.

The day I trekked out to see Karl Simmerling, president of Vancouver Timber Services, I found him forklifting dozens of big Douglas fir timbers—fatter than railroad ties and five times as long—onto a semitrailer flatbed truck sporting Washington state plates. And although I'd called ahead the previous week, booked a precious day care day, and fought traffic in the pouring rain all the way from Bowen Island to this muddy salvage yard, he wasn't very happy to see me.

"I told you I was loading a truck today, James," Simmerling said gruffly, just after shaking my hand.

"You did?" Clearly, we'd gotten our wires crossed.

"The only reason I have any time for you at all is because I have my helper here right now," he scolded. "I can only give you a few minutes."

"Well, show me the goods, then," I replied.

The goods—a stash of two-by-twelve-inch Douglas fir beams, some eight feet long, some twenty feet long—were neatly stacked on the top third of a small mountain of timbers. A few had small notches cut into them; all had holes where iron spikes and screws once bound them together. Liberated from an old-growth rain forest somewhere on Vancouver Island, likely in the 1920s or so (Simmerling didn't volunteer exactly when or where), in their last life, these mighty beams supported the roof of one of the huge sawmills that once dotted the coast. And if the planets aligned, within a matter of days, they'd be making their way over to Bowen, where they'd do the same job for me.

At Dan Parke's suggestion, I'd called Simmerling a few weeks back in search of reclaimed Douglas fir. If there was an obvious place in my plan to use salvaged timber, the roof was it: Parke's drawings specified long beams that extend over the front, south-facing side of the building in a grand and dramatic upward-sweeping overhang. Since they'd be exposed and in a high-profile spot, ideally they'd be clear-grain rafters with few knots.

I could have picked up the phone and had the rafters dropped on Lot 55 within days—but they'd have come straight out of a clear-cut. "I'd try to find some reclaimed wood for that spot," Parke had recommended.

Simmerling had the recycled stuff here, for a price. He deals exclusively in reclaimed Douglas fir—his business card reads "real old wood"—and lots of it. On the phone the previous week, he'd quoted nine dollars a linear foot for a stack of suitable planks his crew had extracted from the balcony of a high-school gymna sium that was being dismantled as part of an earthquake upgrade. The price seemed a little steep, but that was to be expected. I'd already had a taste of the labor required to remove and de-nail wood on a small scale—the cheap stuff in my carport—and this material was of an entirely different pedigree. This fir was massive; it demanded flatbed trucks and cranes. I had decided that spending a premium on recycled wood was just the right thing to do, and I elected not to run the numbers, at least not right away. First I needed to see it.

Doing so was a mistake. Because the moment Simmerling led me through his collection, past a stack of scrolled timbers that, a few decades back, supported a passenger walkway in a Canadian National railway station—once he sent me up a rain-slicked bundle of stacked fir to see the beams in question, well, that's when I fell hard for the stuff. In this era of mass-produced commodified everything, I'm as seduced by authenticity as any-one else. Unlike the bundles of wood down in Big Box land,

Simmerling's product has a soul and a story to tell. And it was calling my name.

These aren't the gymnasium bleachers. Simmerling had sold that shipment three days earlier while I was awaiting my engineer's sign-off on the plans. ("Don't ever do that," chided the reclaimed-timber baron. "Tell your engineer to make it work.") No, these rafters had come out of that sawmill. The clear-grained planks were a half-inch thicker than what I'd get from Home Depot, and I'd need more of them because they were shorter. I'd need to overlap or "sister" them to get my length, which would add to the price. But this wood would be worth it. Or so I told myself.

I was in love with the lumber, yes, but more practical impulses were also driving me. Old wood of the right dimension and length doesn't come through salvage yards all the time. And by this point, I was simply desperate to get construction underway.

The first nail had yet to go in, I was burning through cash, and my panic level was rising. This project was about how to do things differently, but I was feeling the same money-and-time crunch that I imagine just about every builder does on just about every construction project. Elle's grandfather, Henry King Nourse, Jr., was a well-known Bay Area contractor—his contributions to the city include the original domestic terminal building at San Francisco International Airport. Elle tells me that he had a management philosophy that I could learn from: "I don't get ulcers. I give other people ulcers."

Unlike Grandpa Hal, I've had gastritis on and off since the start of my turbo professional life; although it settled down when we moved to Bowen, I could feel it flaring up again as the weeks ticked by. I knew that if I didn't snap up Simmerling's foot-wide beauties, someone else would. He would load them onto the next southbound flatbed that pulled into his muddy yard. If I didn't move decisively, they'd wind up in some soulless Microsoft millionaire's ceiling. Nine dollars a foot—whatever, it was time to be bold.

"I'll take it," I declared. "I'll need sixteen of the twenty-footers and the same number of eights. Write it up, fax me the invoice, and I'll send a check over with my truck driver next week."

"Great," said my matchmaker. He smiled, shook my hand, stroked his goatee, and returned to his forklift.

* * *

The invoice arrived a few days later, and it read like a Dear John letter. With taxes, my secondhand studio rafters ran $4,840.92. I'd also need another $651 for delivery, plus easily a grand's worth of labor to clean them up with a belt sander. Grand total, about $6,400. Just to support the roof. Of a studio. I swallowed hard. Simmerling had always been honest with me about the bottom line, but seeing it on paper was startling. Real old wood was real expensive. It was more than I'd allocated for all the lumber in the whole studio, and I should have figured that out to begin with.

To gain some perspective, I called a local clear-cut lumber retailer—the place I suspect supplied the studs, joists, and trusses hidden behind the drywall in my own home. The salesman said he could get me clear-cut-harvested rafters in twenty-four hours for just $753.03 plus delivery. On this one small piece of my tenuously financed project, the "right thing to do"—going with recycled wood—would set me back an additional four grand. Were I running a big, blank-check high-profile project, I'd happily sign on the dotted line. The PR value alone would be worth the extra bills. But the Eco-Shed wasn't that kind of deal. Just as I'd done with my local roast gone wrong, I consulted my household controller for guidance.

"I dunno, hon, it seems like your decision is already made for you," Elle said when I explained the situation. "I'm sure this guy's timbers are gorgeous. And yeah, they're reclaimed. But they're not for us. They're for rich people."

I flashed to a Microsoft Excel product-group manager shrugging while my timbers vanished into the ceiling of his eco-savvy lakefront retreat. "I know, I know," I said. I knew I had to call Simmerling, who would probably tear me a new one for wasting still more of his time. He'd probably already shuffled his stock around in anticipation of my flatbed truck. There was only one thing to do.

"Tell him you're really sorry you wasted his time, that you didn't know any better," Elle suggested. "Just play the doofus card."

In other words, just be myself. I improvised a bit, cowardly pinning part of the blame on Parke, who had nothing to do with my error. "Listen, I've spent the past hour with my architect going over the budget, and I am really sorry, but I just don't think I can make this work. I only have seventy-five thousand dollars for my whole project, soup to nuts, so no matter how I play it, now that I see the total, I've had to accept that this is out of my league."

There was silence at the other end of the line. At least he was professional. "Oh well, this isn't the first time it's happened," he said. I knew what he meant.

I was heartbroken. Simmerling was my best hope to incorporate at least some reclaimed lumber into a structure that would otherwise, by practical necessity, be born of a clear-cut. That's the unadvertised reality behind just about every $1.87 two-by-four stud on the rack down at your Home Depot; it's where the thousands of feet of lumber in the walls of my house originated.

Almost every day I can look out from my porch and see tugs towing football-field-sized booms of cedar and fir to the mills at the top end of Howe Sound. It's a marine parade that never ends. Despite decades of protest campaigns and a number of high-profile victories—such as the February 2006 agreement that preserves five million acres of British Columbia's Great Bear Rainforest—clear-cutting remains such standard industry practice that it's very difficult in these parts to buy framing lumber of any other kind.

Unfortunately, there would be nothing particularly eco about the walls of the Eco-Shed. Before I picked up the phone to order a bundle of off-the-shelf studs and joists, I wanted to know what I was getting myself into. I already knew that clear-cutting was bad news from a biodiversity perspective (just ask the salmon, the spotted owl, the caribou, etc.), but was take-no-prisoners-style logging heating up the planet, too?

I confess that I had my doubts. After all, trees take up carbon dioxide from the atmosphere by way of photosynthesis—they stash CO_2 in their tissue. And when Joe Lumberjack and his friend Sawmill Bill parlay a hillside worth of spruce and fir into so-called long-life wood products—such as a home's studs, joists, trusses, and flooring—they don't release that banked CO_2 back into the atmosphere. At my place, it's still right here, all around me, just behind the drywall.

Meanwhile, as I was writing this book at the tail end of spring, on some remote devastated British Columbia mountainside a cash-starved college student was tucking a finger-sized seedling into a patch of dirt—one of the two hundred million sprouts planted on government-owned land each year to replace every tree cut down, as provincial law requires. And every one of those young, vigorously growing saplings is, at this moment, enthusiastically sucking my SUV's carbon dioxide out of the atmosphere. Right?

Well, yes, but not as quickly as I'd imagined. "Young trees just don't store carbon as effectively as old-growth trees do," explains Faisal Moola, the director of science for the Vancouver-based David Suzuki Foundation. "By turning a forest—typically an old-growth forest—into long-lived forest products, you are significantly truncating the capacity of that forest to store carbon."

It turns out that standard-issue *Lorax*-style forestry kicks up a great deal of carbon dioxide tucked away in an unexpected place: dirt. "Logging releases a lot of carbon through mechanical disturbance of the forest soil," Moola says. "Much of the carbon that is released is not in the form of the biomass destroyed—the slash left behind—but rather the pools of soil below the ground that are opened up when the trees are taken out." That's in addition to the inevitable emissions generated by the processing, milling, and transporting of the lumber.

We aren't about to stop cutting down trees, of course; many building materials, particularly steel and concrete, are far more emissions intensive than lumber. But we need to embrace what Moola calls "carbon-conservative" practices. "We need to log in a way that leaves as much of the carbon in the system as possible," he says.

Mainly, this means harvesting less frequently. Instead of cutting down replanted forests every 40 years, we might let them stand for 150 or 200 years, he suggests. "When you lengthen this so-called rotation rate, you are improving the capacity of the system to store carbon," Moola says. It also means more gentle logging methods that do not disturb the critical soil pools. "Leave large areas of old-growth alone," he says. "Log less; use reclaimed and recyclable materials more, particularly for short-lifespan products like tissues. It is harder to do in terms of building materials, but we all have to reduce our footprint."

Once again, it boils down to the now-familiar but largely still-futile appeal that crosses the grain of entitlement, economies of scale, and the cultural value so many of us still ascribe to cathedral ceilings, great rooms, and other wide open spaces within our homes: "Build something smaller."

* * *

There are alternatives to clear-cut lumber other than high-end reclaimed timber. I could have borrowed a pickup truck and worked my way through a string of local building materials salvage yards. Eventually, over a period of perhaps weeks, I could have scrounged up the right number of studs I needed, in the right lengths, to assemble my Eco-Shed. But I didn't have the time or energy. A more realistic option would have been to specify so-called certified wood—that is, by and large, harvested with the kind of sustainable logging practices that Moola refers to.

A number of these certification programs exist, but the only one with real teeth is managed by the Forest Stewardship Council, a nonprofit organization based in Bonn, Germany, and active in forty countries, including Canada and the United States. In a nutshell, the FSC tree logo does for lumber what the Energy Star label does for appliances and windows—it lets you know you've made the greener choice. An FSC stamp guarantees that the wood adheres to a set of ten principles of forest stewardship, including a set of kinder, gentler harvesting practices. FSC-certified foresters work selectively—leaving tracts of trees intact—and pay close attention to issues such as erosion, wildlife habitat, streams, and lakes. The program was set up to protect biodiversity long before greenhouse gas emissions really hit the radar screen, but it certainly advances carbon-conservative practices along the way. It was still the best option for a wannabe green guy like me with a modest shopping list of long-life wood products.

There was only one problem: There was none for me to buy.

Although my province contains more than 1.5 million acres of FSC-certified forestlands, that number is a thin 1 percent of the total land out this way open to logging. At the time of this writing, every sustainably harvested two-by-four stud milled in this part of the world came out of a pair of sawmills located in the southeastern corner of the province, a hundred-odd miles due north of Idaho. The two plants, owned and operated by Tembec, a $3.5 billion forest products company based in western Quebec, crank 'em out like chopsticks. And just about every last plank winds up on a flatbed railcar heading the same direction Karl Simmerling's is going: south, to the United States.

To be fair, I could have picked up the phone and ordered some FSC lumber for my Bowen Island Eco-Shed—the trouble is, I'd have ended up with a few pieces left over. "If you wanted certified two-by-fours, I could probably get them to you," said Moriah Stutt, owner of MoCo Sustainable Connections, a local FSC brokerage company and wholesaler. "But only 294 pieces at a time."

I hit the phone in search of a retailer that could get me carbon-conservative framing lumber in sub-railcar quantities. The nearest Home Depot had no idea what I was talking about. Ditto several other local chains. Four or five calls later, I hit pay dirt: "By coincidence, I brought in two packs of FSC lumber this week," said the head buyer for Dick's, a local mom-and-pop outfit. "I've got a package of two-by-fours in sixteen-foot length, and a package of two-by-tens, also sixteens."

They were not exactly the dimension I was looking for, but I still felt as if I'd won the lottery. "How did you happen to come across that?" I asked.

"I called it in to show it to my sales team and talk with them about it," the buyer said. "Isn't that wild that you're asking me for it, out of the blue?"

Parke's plans specified sixty-nine two-by-sixes and a couple dozen two-by-fours of various lengths. Dick's had me covered on the two-by-fours, but the ten-inchers wouldn't work. They were too wide.

"Are you ordering any more certified wood anytime soon?" I asked.

"Well, this was kind of a one-shot deal," the buyer said. "There's just not much demand for this out there."

I made another round of calls to confirm there was no other FSC wood at retail within a hundred miles or so. Nothing. Then my high-school algebra kicked in to save the day, just as Dad always assured me it would. When I sat down with my graphing calculator, I discovered that four inches plus six inches—again, the two widths we need to frame up the Eco-Shed—add up to ten inches.

I could use the FSC wood from Dick's after all. We just needed to set up a table saw in the yard and feed those suckers through, one board at a time. If Tembec was shuffling all of its sustainably harvested spruce and fir directly out of the country, then I'd tap into one of the few bundles that fell off the truck and remill the boards right here in the driveway.

It was subversive but brilliant. It was also a bargain: the carbon-conservative FSC wood only set me back two hundred dollars more than the regular stuff. For once, the sustainable alternative did not cost me many times more than the original flavor. There was a snag, though: I still needed to order the clear-cut-grade two-by-twelve roof joists. I was a day or two from approving the order, with a heavy heart, when I bumped into Jeremy Galpin, my vegan, Volkswagen-truck-driving carpenter, down at the island's organic grocery store. "I've got a line on your two-by-twelves," he said.

"What do you mean?" I asked. "I've already got those included in the order." Having dismissed reclaimed lumber for budget reasons, I'd reluctantly added a bundle of clear-cut grade joists to the Dick's delivery.

"Well, these are recycled," he replied.

When it comes to secondhand wood, it pays to shop around—especially when someone else has all the relevant phone numbers on speed dial. Galpin's source, a fellow VW enthusiast, kept his lumber stash an hour's drive deeper into the suburbs than Simmerling. Not only would he get me the fir rafters I needed—a full set of twenty footers and eights, remilled from a railroad trestle on Vancouver Island—he'd clean them up and deliver them to my job site. They would still cost more than standard clear-cut grade lumber would run me, but not a whole lot more—a price I could feel good about. "I've seen his operation," said Galpin. "I was really impressed. It's good stuff."

I snapped it up. Since I'd already secured a source of FSC plywood that another friend had stashed away elsewhere on the island, my lumber order was now fully dialed. Thanks to persistence, detective work, and sheer dumb luck in the face of a crushing deadline, every stick of wood in the Eco-Shed would be carbon conservative. My conscience was as clear as the old-growth grain on a nineteenth-century railroad trestle timber. All I needed now was a floor.

* * *

Back on Granville Island, at the genesis of the Eco-Shed, Helen Goodland had discouraged me from running my own show. At issue, she'd explained, is the "critical path"—the tight choreography of tradesmen who must come and go in a specific sequence and materials that must be waiting for them when they arrive. The critical path isn't just about scheduling; it's about understanding how long things take, how they come together, where the bottlenecks lie, and having the right materials on hand at the right time. To successfully navigate this maze, it helps to have a Wikipedic knowledge of codes and construction practices. And surprise, surprise, I found this out the hard way.

Greg Sims specifies and installs heating, ventilation, and air-conditioning systems—crucial components of a high-performance building like the Eco-Shed. Sims came over one day to take a look at Parke's construction drawings and recommend a heating strategy. Although the studio would be passively warmed by the winter sun whenever possible, it would also need primary and backup heating systems. We ruled out electric baseboard heaters straight away; although the registers warm the rooms of our main house that our high-efficiency woodstove can't reach, they are notorious electricity hogs. And since conservation and performance rule my Eco-Shed world, I'd instructed Sims to strike them from his list of options.

My man came up with something far better: in-slab hydronic heat. We'd warm the building via a network of hot-water tubing laid down in the new slab; warm fluid circulating within would keep the floor at a constant temperature with a minimal investment of energy. Our plan was to dig out the sarcophagus rubble, add a fresh layer of crushed rock, tamp it down billiard-table flat with a plate compactor, lay down a grand or so worth of rigid-foam insulation, then top that with a lattice of rebar. Sims would then zip-tie a few hundred feet of plastic tubing to the rebar. He'd snake it across the space in a carefully planned maze of tight loops, which would all begin and end inside a small corner space that we'd set aside as our utilities room. There, a small pump would constantly circulate the fluid through a baby electric hot-water tank pressed into service as a boiler.

"You don't need an actual boiler for a space this size," Sims said.

He worked his calculator for a moment or two. "I'm going to get you a twenty-five-gallon tank, a little guy, a Campbell's Soup can," he continued. "And I'm going to remove one of the two elements, so you just have a forty-five-hundred-watt element keeping that fluid warm."

"It will take a lot of juice to get the slab up to comfortable temperature," Sims explained. "But with all this insulation, it'll take only a trickle of energy to keep it there."

The plan sounded perfect. And as a backup for those three-day-long winter power failures caused by the kind of global-warming-related extreme weather events we seem to be seeing more of these days, I'd ordered a small high-efficiency woodstove.

Sims would tie down his tubing just before the concrete pour. I had serious misgivings about tearing out and redoing the slab—as we've already learned, atmospherically speaking, concrete is exceedingly bad news—but knew I could never reach my passive-solar goals without foam insulation underfoot.

And then I stumbled across a new island start-up with the improbable name of Eco-Mix Concrete. Although the branding smacks of greenwashing—the dubious PR practice of trying to cast a sustainable glow over a mightily undeserving product or industry—in this case, proprietor Dennis Dallas is on to something. For one thing, his equipment can mix the material on-site in small batches, avoiding the high delivery costs and greenhouse gases associated with giant trucks coming over from the mainland. He can also tweak his concrete's recipe in a greener direction.

I knew that concrete could be mixed with a higher percentage of fly ash—a waste product scrubbed from the stacks of coal-fired electric power stations. The material works well as a binder and can displace a certain amount of that rather unfortunate cement in the mix. I e-mailed Dallas to ask if his equipment could handle a small pour high in fly ash. "We just finished a job and have some dry mix left over that is 40 percent fly ash," he wrote back. "I think we'd have enough for your project."

Dan Parke confirmed that a 40 percent fly-ash mix is indeed impressive—as far as concrete goes, it's about as green as one can get without serious trade-offs in stability, workability, and curing time. "I'll take it," I replied. Dallas said he'd prep the slab, install the foam and rebar, then come back to pour after Greg Sims had tied down his hydronic tubing. We braided our critical paths together.

Everything went as smooth as Jif: Dallas laid down the rebar on a Wednesday, loaded his truck with his leftover high-fly-ash dry mix, and told me he needed to pour it before the weekend. I called in Sims. And that's when I veered right off my critical path and straight into the critical roadside ditch.

My heating guy showed up with his supplies and promptly went away again. "I can't tie the tubing down onto rebar," Sims told me. "There aren't enough attachment points; I was hoping to see a layer of ten-inch square welded-steel mesh in there. Call me back when you get it down and we'll be right over." I knew the material he had in mind: they stocked it at the island's building center.

"I'll get it done this afternoon," I told Sims. I knew he was fitting me in between far more lucrative jobs.

I rushed out, bought a few sheets, plopped it in the slab atop the rebar, and called him back.

His voice mail picked up. "Sorry," said the automated attendant. "There is no more room for messages."

Uh oh.

I tried again a day later. Same thing. The only number I had for him was evidently jammed with other obligations. We were fast closing in on the end of the week, when Dallas had scheduled my job. Could he put me off a day or so if needed? I explained the situation.

"The thing is, James, I've already loaded my truck with your dry mix. The only way to get it out of there is to mix it and pour it. And I've got another job on Monday that needs a different recipe, so one way or another, I'm unloading my truck this weekend."

The message was clear: If I didn't get back on my critical path before Monday, Dallas would pour my eco-concrete right in my eco-driveway and send me the bill.

I asked Parke for guidance. "I think it might be time to leave a note on Greg's front door," he said. "A six-pack of beer wouldn't hurt, either."

I looked up Sims's address and drove the Lexus over. No one was home, so I taped a large note, in Panic Bold Italic typeface—punctuated with the smiley-face icon featuring a capital O for the mouth and hair standing on end—on the front door. Late Friday night, just as I was glumly scouting out a space to receive a big, slushy, useless pile of eco-concrete, Sims called back. He'd been away at a conference that he'd neglected to mention. He came over the next morning and did his thing, and the eco-concrete came down the chute minutes later. The planets aligned just in time.

The lesson: Assume nothing. Ask endless probing and tedious questions at every stage of the process—even if your five-year-old is crying hysterically in the background because your three-year-old has just bitten her on the forearm. Get as involved in the nitty gritty as possible.

I lined up my electrical contractor and the spray-foam insulation dude and ordered steel roofing and a gigantic rainwater-harvesting cistern. The Eco-Shed's walls were even going up—I'd taken delivery of my FSC lumber and sheathing, and Galpin quickly framed up the building, at long last ratcheting nuts down onto those once-forlorn lag bolts.

The time had come to order what might have been the most crucial pieces of my passive-solar puzzle. They could either make or break my high-performance goals, and I would be living with the consequences for decades. Unfortunately, in the grand green scheme of things, they are perhaps the most vexing bits and pieces of my eco-puzzle to try to figure out.

I'm talking about the windows—the fruits of an industry that remains frustratingly shrouded in mystique and technical gobbledygook. "There needs to be a window support group," said Helen Goodland at the Light House Sustainable Building Centre. "It is the absolute worst area to navigate. It is quite interesting, because insulation companies are great, the lumber companies are offering FSC wood, the paint companies have done wonderful things removing volatile organic compounds; all these sectors have really got the bit between their teeth.

"But the window folks have been the biggest problem. It is not just that they can't be bothered; it is also the misinformation they're putting out there."

I had some homework to do on a crucial piece of my project and not much time to do it. Given the unconventional nature of this project—and my stubborn refusal to compromise on my green goals—my original spring completion estimate had proven wildly unrealistic. Despite the project's small size, everything about it has been long-lead-time this and special-order that. I was now hard up against the ropes of my deadline. I knew I needed high-performance windows, but I didn't have much time to research them; even Dan Parke was struggling. This we did know: As with all things green, the key is to look for third-party certification; for windows, that system is Energy Star.

Following Helen Goodland's original advice, I wouldn't order anything less than Energy Star windows, but beyond that, who knows? Trying to compare one company's products with another's was like solving a cipher; brochures and Web sites were full of jargon and arcane three-dimensional graphs. None of it made much sense, and unfortunately, delivery time had quickly risen to the top of my selection criteria. A multinational windows company with impressive logistics, field support, "just-in-time" manufacturing, and massive marketing budgets—just for fun, let's call it Pellandersen—could get me my glass in three to four weeks. A second, much smaller company, might make a better window, but they'd need at least two months to do it. *Two months!*

Unfortunately, my inner turbo got the best of me once again, and soon enough, the Pellandersen sales guy—let's call him Rick Slickpane—was sitting down at my kitchen table with a stack of brochures and a miniature model window. He'd come to tell Parke and me about his goods and close a deal.

Slickpane went on at some length about how the frames are built; what the spacers between the panes are made of and why; what kind of finishes and color options he could order up; handle and hinge options; what it used to be like in the Wild West days before liability drove all window-design decisions; how solid the warranty was, etc., etc. It was a meandering stream of unadulterated sales-speak buddy bullshit. After he deflected one or two probing questions, I concluded that he didn't have the slightest idea how his product stacked up against the other guy's when it came to the only measure that mattered to me: performance.

I had limited and expensive child-care support, and I had a set of windows to order. I simply didn't have time to listen to canned "creation myths." It kept coming, though, and my blood pressure inched up. Just before the kids—who had been playing upstairs with a babysitter—began their daily prelunch meltdown, I interrupted Slickpane's canned script.

"Look," I blurted out, "to be honest, I don't care about all that stuff. I want to know how well your windows work. What are the R-values? Do they leak air? If so, how much?"

He smiled. But I wasn't finished.

"What I need from you is hard data on performance, in a format I can understand and compare with the other guys. And if you don't have it, I need you to find someone who does, OK?"

"Absolutely," he assured me. "I'll get you that right away." A few days later, less than twenty-four hours remaining before the order cutoff deadline for the week, Slickpane e-mailed me three documents: The first included a poor-quality scan of twenty-seven pages of charts and cross-sections and wire-frame diagrams; the second contained an even worse scan of a photocopy of the sticker that ships on a window; the third was a sales contract for $6,362.77 that just needed my signature and a credit card number.

I needed the windows on the job site yesterday. But I still had no idea what I was getting other than a twenty-year history of blah blah blah. I had a quick powwow with Dan Parke, who had visited the Energy Star Web site and compared the quick-turnaround Pellandersen with the specialty, longer-lead-time Brand Y. There it was, the magic number I needed—an independently tested measurement called the E-Rating that rolled together a window's overall performance based on solar heat gain, heat loss, and—hello, Helen Goodland!—air leakage.

Surprise, surprise; the small company's glass was more than twice as efficient as the stuff Slickpane was hoping to sell me. His company books more than $1 billion worth of business each year. It's the same outfit that spends millions each year on television and magazine advertising and that could get me my glass at turbo speed: three weeks, tops.

"I'm now officially in a hurry to build this," I told Parke. "People always are. The schedule rules the world, and it backs us into corners and forces us to make compromises. The difference between these guys and those guys is another four weeks; that's time that I don't have, but then again, I'll be living with these windows for years."

There was only one thing to do. I told Slickpane to take a hike. And it's a damn good thing that I did, too. Because it turned out that the big-name windows I had wisely passed over are poorly suited to a passive-solar building; they're designed to keep the sun's heat out, to avoid cooking a home's occupants in summer. Sweltering indoors won't be an issue for me, because in the warmer months, my shed's giant roof overhangs will keep the sun out. These windows are built for the mass market, and the mass-market consumer doesn't have six-foot wings coming off the side of his or her roof.

My Eco-Shed's windows will be made of fiberglass, a material that shrinks and expands at roughly the same rate as the glass, keeping stress off seals. It doesn't conduct heat very well, won't rot, isn't poisonous should it burn, and won't grow mold. The building envelope was good to go: The walls were up, the rafters were complete, sheathing was on, and the glass was in the pipe. Now all we had to do was put it together.

9

Tankosaurus

"Now that's more like it," Lexus thought to herself as the man carefully hand-buffed the final few inches of her golden-pearl clear-coat paint. It had been a very long time since she'd enjoyed a day quite this luxurious. A very long time indeed.

She had spent more than two years quietly suffering at the grubby hands of small children; the pampering was long overdue. Her owners had specified the full $289.95 "magic detailing" treatment, and dear Lord did she ever need it. She hadn't visited a spa—hell, she'd hardly been *washed*—since the day before she was loaded onto a truck in California and driven to her new home. She'd lost count of the indignities she'd suffered in the interim.

Two sets of chronically drool-soaked little fingers—often sticky with fruit-leather goo—had pawed her leather trim and windows. Two pairs of muddy rubber boots had kicked at her seats. At one point, the smaller of the two urchins had seized a ballpoint pen and scrawled a long blue line down the tan leather of her passenger-side rear door panel. Obscene quantities of juice, cookies, goldfish crackers, sand, fairy glitter, and yogurt had been ground into her floor mats. Putrid diapers had been changed in her cargo compartment, which at various points had also hosted a laundry list of decidedly nonluxury goods, such as bags of concrete mix, rounds of firewood, rolls of galvanized-aluminum deer fencing, and a random assortment of discarded objects scavenged off the side of the road.

None of this was supposed to happen to Lexus. She had been designed to carry golf clubs, gourmet organic groceries from Whole Foods, perhaps a fresh-baked pie and some flowers from the local farmer's market, maybe a couple crates of Bordeaux. With her walnut trim and fine appointments, she was intended for a select few who had *earned* the right to drive her. She was for people of considerable means. She preferred full-service high-octane. She wasn't Old Navy; she was Prada. And she was most certainly *not* interested in small children of any persuasion. After all, gaudy car seats have their place in the world, and that place is the back of a wagon or minivan, behind a tacky Winnie the Pooh sunshade.

But everything was going to be better now. The man had spent the entire day lavishing the kind of thoughtful attention on Lexus that she felt she deserved. He'd steamed her six-cylinder engine, cleaned and reconditioned her leather seats. He'd magically erased the ballpoint pen. The man had vacuumed and shampooed all her carpets and mats. He'd scrubbed and polished her glass, tires, rims, door jambs, instrument cluster, and every vent and crevice in her dashboard. He'd spent an entire day purging all evidence that a young family had ever buckled themselves into her six-way-adjustable power seats. She looked and smelled much as she had seven years before, when she rolled off the line at a spotless Toyota plant near the northern tip of the island of Kyushu, Japan. Just as she was then, she was positively glowing today.

But the owner had a hidden agenda. The engine shampoo and hand-wax were not a reward for humiliations endured; they were a kiss-off. This day of automotive pampering was the equivalent of taking a girlfriend out to an expensive restaurant and dumping her over dessert. The owner had already listed Lexus for sale and hoped to close a deal within days.

Lexus had no idea it was coming.

* * *

I drummed the steering wheel and sang along to the radio, as the sun poured in through the moon roof. It was mid-May, and we were on our way to four days of spring fun and sun at a tucked-away beach place on Vancouver Island. Our spirits were riding high. It was a thrill to run from deadlines and editors and stress and green-building carousels, but that wasn't the only reason I felt so jubilant. This was our last hurrah with the RX 300. With a few keystrokes and ultimately a signature on the line, I was about to radically shrink our family's carbon footprint, consequences be damned.

Our wheels were up on Craigslist, and we already had four or five prospects lined up. Our plan was simple: We'd hoped to unload the seventeen-mile-per-gallon beast on one of the many nearby urbanites who still think pickups, minivans, and suvs—technically, they're called light trucks—are de rigueur. The stats reveal they're out there: According to the U.S. Department of Commerce, in 2006 Americans purchased about 105 million new light trucks and ninety-three million passenger cars. The spread narrowed the following year, but only slightly; about 102 million big rigs rolled off the nation's lots in 2007, compared to ninety-two million cars. Although these numbers were discouraging in the grander picture, they propped up my selfish short-term agenda quite nicely: get rid of the car before the market catches up to the headlines.

The replacement we had in mind was a subcompact. It weighed less than half what the Lexus did and wouldn't haul much more than the four of us and a couple bags of groceries. And that was just fine, because we could do with a little Flechas-Castillo-style austerity in our lives anyway. Buying a tiny, sporty car would give us the vehicular equivalent of a gastric bypass operation; we'd feel fuller faster, which would naturally help curb our consumer appetites. We wouldn't buy as much vacuous crap, I reasoned, because we'd have no way of getting it home. But most important, we'd slash that naggingly large transportation footprint. In one relatively easy move, without driving any less than we did already—a small amount in itself—by my calculations, we'd cut 1.64 tons of carbon dioxide from our lives each year.

And, uh, pass them on to someone else.

But before we even booked the first driveway show-and-tell, we were taking this one last road trip—a weekend family getaway with all the crap our rig could carry. We were off to the rustic beach place where I spent many summers as a young lad, hunting for garter snakes, swimming in the ocean, and piecing together elaborate driftwood forts on the beach (hey, I was into reclaimed wood *way* before it was trendy). The weather was incredible, the kids were pumped, the tunes were cranked, and everyone was giddy as our golden-pearl rig smoothly accelerated up an all-but-empty highway. We'd packed the Lexus to the headlining with wine, food, and inflatable vinyl beach toys. As the miles unspooled, we felt the bonds of the daily grind releasing. The moment captured the original joy of motoring—the promise of total freedom, the escape from workaday worries.

A large insect splatted across the windshield, leaving a bright yellow smear. "Guess we shoulda had this thing detailed *after* we took it away for the weekend," I said to Elle, smiling.

"Oh, whatever; bugs wash off," she replied. "That's the easy part; the hard part was erasing years' worth of kid grunge. Whoever buys this thing won't find so much as a DNA strand of evidence that we ever even owned it."

"I wonder if we'll be able to sell it by next weekend."

"I sure hope so," Elle said. "Let's cue up some of those prospects!"

With the cruise control engaged and Duncan and Sabrina grooving to the Dixie Chicks, I glanced over at the dash. There, a central LCD display showed me current outside temperature, trip distance, elapsed time, current mileage, and settings for air-conditioning, the sound system, and so on. I was supposed to think of it as my vehicle's electronic nerve center, but the display conveyed largely pointless information. It was designed to reassure me that I was in control, that all systems were functioning normally.

I was the first to notice the trouble.

"Hey, the screen is blank," I said matter-of-factly.

"What?! Oh you've *got* to be kidding," Elle cried.

I was not. It *was* blank, except for the digital clock in the corner.

"What the hell is this car doing?"

After wringing our hands for the better part of a year over our vehicle's gigantic ecological footprint but doing nothing for fear of offending the loving father who gave it to us, we had finally mustered up the resolve to downsize. We had interested buyers lined up. And the damn thing appeared to be broken.

"This can't be happening!" wailed Elle. "What is it with this car?"

Actually, I had a theory.

* * *

My mother was nine months pregnant with me when Dad dragged her out to see Stanley Kubrick's *2001: A Space Odyssey.* Ever since, I've never heard the end of what a torture it was to be crammed into a seat in a packed theater for two hours, especially during the final twenty minutes—a loud and seemingly unending sequence of deep-space travel, during which I kicked my mother repeatedly in the bladder.

Clearly, I ruined the movie for Mum. But my first science-fiction experience somehow lodged in my prenatal brain, and every now and then, themes and scenes from the film seem to pop up in my life. And this is precisely what happened as the Lexus attempted to ruin my vacation.

Midway through the film, astronauts Dave Bowman and Frank Poole retreat into a space pod to discuss the fate of HAL 9000, their ship's onboard computer system. Through the many months of their mission to Jupiter, the artificial intelligence has proven their faithful servant and companion. To them, he is not so much a machine as a trusted member of the crew.

But their electronic colleague has just done something alarming and completely unprecedented: he's made a mistake. Knowing that HAL sees and hears everything said and done onboard the ship, Bowman and Poole seal themselves inside the little soundproof pod to discuss the glitch. It's serious business, and the two humans don't want to hurt their computer's feelings by discussing his failure in front of him. Safely out of HAL's earshot, they consider whether they should disconnect him. But unbeknownst to them, the computer is reading their lips through the porthole. He doesn't like their game plan at all. And he is not about to go quietly.

I knew why the Lexus display was displaying nothing. I also knew why the power windows had just stopped functioning— and why the "door ajar" warning light had just come on, even though all the doors were firmly closed and latched. I knew why the air-conditioning would not respond to its controls. Like HAL 9000, Lexus had been reading our lips. She knew that after years of indignities and injustices, she was no longer wanted. And she was not about to go quietly. What would she do? Would she send us into the ditch? Or worse, silence the Dixie Chicks?

Everything seemed to be working except the windows, air-conditioning, and display. We continued driving, and a half hour or so later, just like that, all systems returned to normal. It was as if nothing had happened. For the rest of the weekend, and on the return drive home, we attempted to replicate the brief digital brownout. No luck. Our wheels were running perfectly. The windows went up and down on command. It was a classic ghost in the machine.

What to do? If we sold the car and the new owner encountered the glitch a day or so later, he or she would bring it straight back to our driveway. That could get messy. But if we disclosed the incident to our prospects in advance, they'd probably pass us by. For all we knew, the problem might never occur again. There was only one ethical thing to do: take the car in to a dealer for a complete checkup. If anyone could find the trouble, it would be the dealer guys. They'd have all the special diagnostic scopes and machines. And they only charged a very reasonable $110 an hour for labor, plus taxes, of course.

Sitting on a cedar log at the beach cottage, while the kids hunted grass snakes nearby, I called for an appointment. The service adviser had never heard of the blank-screen problem before. Of course. "We'll probably want to hang on to it for a few days while we troubleshoot the problem," he said. I pictured dollar signs spinning like the wheels on a slot machine. "Will you be needing a courtesy car, sir?"

"Yeah, this is our only vehicle."

"Well, I'm afraid the soonest our loaner vehicle will be available will be the end of the month."

"The end of the month? That's weeks from now! I'm hoping to put this car on the market and sell it right away." This delay was truly a blow, because emotionally, I'd long since moved on. I'd be stuck living with the girlfriend I'd just dumped.

"I'm very sorry, sir. If you'd like to arrange your own transportation while we are checking over the vehicle, we can see you on Wednesday."

I needed to finalize this split pronto. All I needed to feel good about the transaction was a piece of paper that said everything looked good.

"I'll be there at 9:30," I said.

* * *

I had never before set foot inside a Lexus dealership. In the two years we'd lived on the rock, Chris Leigh, my island's gifted mechanic, had kept our wheels shipshape. Stepping into this showroom felt eerie and unsettling—a space walk into another demographic, a voyeuristic visit to a radically different worldview. I felt as though I'd blundered into a lavish temple dedicated to the most luxurious incarnation of the internal combustion engine and that I had no business being here.

In a bid to attract young overachievers who've pursued far more lucrative careers than mine, the welcome page on this dealer's Web site displays a terrific slogan: "Not Your Father's Lexus." It's a riff on an old Oldsmobile pitch, but it's deliciously appropriate, and the decor in the showroom underscored the irony. I felt as if I'd just stepped into Padre's living room. The whole place was arranged around a circular customer lounge, furnished with dreamy black leather armchairs, complimentary wireless Internet, and a large plasma television screen that was tuned to—of all things—a ladies' bowling competition. A wall display caught my eye, a list of one hundred things every person should do in his or her lifetime. It was the usual breathless *carpe diem* bullshit—fly a helicopter over the Grand Canyon, dance like nobody's watching—that editors at upscale consumer magazines spend a good deal of their time trying to dream up.

Then I reached suggestion number one hundred: "Drive a Lexus."

The placard crystallized my transformation. For so many, the vehicle I was desperately trying to unload represents the pinnacle of a lifetime of striving. To them, it is the Stanley Cup of life, the endgame of a decade of early mornings and late nights spent working the phone, pressing the flesh, and closing the deals. To them, the golden L logo proclaims one thing: "Hey, everyone, check me out."

To me, it meant something else entirely. I've always felt fairly comfortable operating at multiple levels of society—I can rub elbows with venture capitalists when called to do so, and I can PowerPoint with the best of them—but the chasm between that carefully styled sales floor and my present state of mind felt so vast that I couldn't see to the other side. I handed over the keys and caught a ride to the nearest bus stop aboard the dealership's courtesy shuttle, a Lexus LS 460— something of a holy grail for luxury auto enthusiasts; with help from onboard computers and sonar arrays, the car *can actually park itself.* There was a white sticker on the instrument panel, intended only for the driver: "Please be responsible for your own fuel use."

For the next few days, I would be car free. It was easy enough for me to hop the bus back to the ferry dock that afternoon. But once there, the real work would begin. Because the next day, a very warm spring day, I walked Duncan and Sabrina home from day care—a fairly relentless uphill slog, accessorized with lunch boxes and totes of fingerpaint-soiled clothes, not to mention various precious pieces of artwork fashioned with clamshells, popsicle sticks, crepe paper, and clay. Our hands were full; the children were hot, tired, and hungry. At various points, their bodies went limp in protest; they laid on the pavement and sobbed. My son wailed his one-word command, "Carry!" And the moment we stumbled through the doorway, I called the Lexus dealer and begged for my keys.

"I'm very sorry, sir. Our technician has not been able to replicate the problem you experienced," the service adviser said. "We've tried it a number of times, but the car seems to be working great. If we can't see a problem, we can't fix it."

"OK, well, did you hook it up to your machines and run the tests or whatever? Did you check for computer error codes?"

Open the pod bay doors, HAL.

"We did. No codes came up. We can keep trying if you like."

I'm sorry, Dave. I can't do that.

"Let's forget it," I snapped. "For all we know, you could keep it there for a month and check it every day and nothing would happen. And I'd be stuck without a car."

HAL, open the doors!

"That's true, that might be the case," he said. "Right now, it's looking like this is just one of those freak things. The vehicle is running perfectly. There's nothing wrong with it."

I'm sorry, Dave. I can't do that.

* * *

The next day, I set out with the kids on what I billed as an adventure to get the car back from the mechanic. Unfortunately, my charges wised up to my spin sometime ago. They now know what "adventure" means, and it has nothing to do with swashbuckling fun. We'd walk down the hill to the ferry (twenty minutes), ride the boat to the mainland (twenty-five minutes), and dash up a long concrete ramp to the bus (five minutes) that is scheduled to leave within a scant few minutes of our arrival. We'd then ride the bus (thirty minutes), get off and wait (fifteen minutes) for another bus (twenty minutes), then—since auto malls are evidently not well served by public transit—we would walk down four long blocks along a busy road through an office-park hell, over a steep railway overpass, and then down another quarter-mile of blistering sidewalk to the dealership (realistically, forty-five minutes). Suffice to say, it is a trip best undertaken in a vehicle. I am too stubborn (and cheap) to take a cab.

The adventure got off to a rocky start when, with five minutes remaining before the ferry's departure, Sabrina tripped on broken asphalt in front of the island's general store and opened up her knee. Blood streamed down her calf, tears down her face, and wails of agony echoed across the parking lot. I had no Band-Aids, just a flask of water, and no one rushed over to help, so I poured some of it over the gash to clean it out, which only upset her more. "Now my socks are wet! *Whhaaaaaahhhh! Why can't we just drive?!*"

I bundled her up and started carrying her, dragging Duncan along by the hand. "Sweets, I'm so sorry you're hurt. We're going to get the car, remember?"

Great heaving sobs. *"Ohhhhhkkkaayyyy, Dad."*

I patched up the wound with milk and a cookie aboard the *Queen of Capilano*, and within a few minutes, things were looking up. They didn't fall apart again until the second bus. By the time we got off, the kids had had enough of long-haul public transit. We'd just started walking the final four blocks when Sabrina declared she was starving.

I spied a convenience store—I know better than to push my luck in these cases. "How about a little yogurt and juice?" I offered. Twenty minutes later, the incredible journey continued. It was now the middle of the day. The children had run out of patience. Sports cars and suvs blazed past us bound for the auto mall—potential customers, I realized, redlining the final lap of their rally-race test drives. I gripped my kids' hands on the narrow sidewalk, certain that Duncan would at any moment wander into the road. His three-year-old legs were now so exhausted that he was starting to stumble. I threw him up on my shoulders as we mounted the overpass. The sun beat down on me, and he pulled at my ears and hair, giggling. I was drenched in sweat.

We finally stumbled onto the Lexus lot and into the air-conditioned dealership. Smelling blood, four salesmen leapt up and poured out of their offices to try to sell me a car. "Looking for a vehicle, sir?" I swatted them off with a patient smile and dragged the kids with me through the circular home-theater lounge, straight to the service desk to claim my clean-bill-of-health statement.

"Ah, Mr. Glave. Well, we couldn't find anything wrong with your car, so there's no charge. Here's your key. Your vehicle is right over there."

"Where's my paperwork?" I sputtered.

"There isn't any. No work was done, so there's nothing to sign. You're all good to go. Here's your key."

As I cranked the RX 300's ignition, I felt mighty grateful to Padre. I turned the air-conditioning control knob hard to the left, and the perfectly functioning LCD multidisplay obediently responded with the word "cold." The kids were beaming; I put on their favorite DVD. "This feels much better, Dad," said Sabrina. "It sure is nice to have our car back."

"Yeah, peaches," I replied. "I suppose it is."

* * *

Sport-utility vehicles endure in the marketplace simply because we'd like others to believe we need them. With the exception of the odd sea kayak shuttle, I certainly don't often have cause to transport jumbles of bulky sports equipment to remote trailheads—as much as I would like to—and haven't since Elle and I started a family soon after the millennium rolled its odometer. But now and again, I did deeply appreciate what our wheels could do. And in late June, months after our optimistically billed "last hurrah" trip—with the RX 300 hanging around Craigslist long enough to qualify for hall-of-fame status—I still owned the damn thing. And thank God for that. Because although I didn't often need my SUV for "sport," there came a day in the saga of the Eco-Shed when its promised "utility" really came across.

Parke and I had originally planned to stash a good-sized rainwater cistern under the studio's backside eaves. The building's roof is a respectable 576 square feet, and we'd planned to capture every drop of rain falling on it and funnel it directly into an adjacent storage tank. The tank would, in turn, deliver the harvested water to our neighboring organic veggie garden via gravity feed. I measured the space and threw down my nearly exhausted MasterCard for the biggest tank I could find.

Then one day the beast arrived. It was not just large; it was enormous. It was a certifiable Tankosaurus: eight feet tall and just as wide, capable of stashing 2,400 gallons of potable *agua*. To put the Tankosaurus into neighborhood scale, the previous weekend my friend Jeff had installed a small rainwater cistern in his front yard. He was tired of his ugly rain barrels, and y'know, these things are all the rage on Bowen Island these days.

I helped Jeff muscle his modest rectangular plastic box into the hole he'd dug for it tucked under his front porch. He was very proud of his upgraded capacity, and rightly so. Now he'd be watering his veggies well after the irrigation bans kicked in. Like me, Jeff's a smart guy. But then he drove up to my place and fixed his eyes on the $1,700 behemoth that had just been delivered to my yard. I wasn't in the car with him, but Jeff's response reportedly echoed that of Arthur Dent, who, in a classic Douglas Adams sci-fi novel, glances up to see a fleet of alien ships about to vaporize Planet Earth and screams, "What the hell's that!?"

Yeah, mine is bigger. Sorry, man, that's how it goes. Because when our mayor orders us to stop watering our gardens in the broiling hot summers that doubtless lie ahead, my organic blueberries are going to be doing just fine. And yours? Well, let's hope for the best, Jeff. Thanks to the Tankosaurus, I'll be rocking the hundred-meter diet clear through to Thanksgiving. When it comes to rainwater storage capacity, size really does matter. And fortunately for me, I also still had a big-scale theme going on in the driveway in the form of my SUV. Because in a moment of water tank panic, I would come to need it.

* * *

The Tankosaurus Saga began the moment I took out a measuring tape to confirm that my new, enormous, nonreturnable plastic cistern would tuck neatly under the Eco-Shed's rear eaves as planned. And discovered that it wouldn't. I had the specs right but hadn't factored in the height of the raised pedestal we'd build with stacked rock and gravel fill. The only reason to keep it there alongside the studio—instead of burying the thing, or hiding it, as most people do—was that I wanted to distribute the water via gravity feed, instead of a pump. This was part of my scheme to keep the Eco-Shed's electrical power needs as low as possible. If the tank wouldn't fit in the only place where this could be accomplished, then I could tuck it anywhere. Hell, I could hide it way out in the woods—all it would take was more pipe.

It took Jeremy Galpin to show me the ideal spot. My carpenter took me under my deck, pointed to the steep slope hard up against the house, and said, "I'd tuck it in right there." The measuring tape agreed.

* * *

At five o'clock the next morning, a Saturday, I began hacking out an eight-foot-wide platform in the steep incline that falls sharply away from the deck under the front side of my home's foundation. My plan was to build an eight-foot-wide terrace hard up against the side of the house using a cut-and-fill approach: I'd notch into the slope and deposit the removed material on the downhill side, where I'd retain it with a three- or four-foot-high wall of stacked rock. The terrain sweeping below is classic Bowen Island topography: loose shale and crumbling rock held in place by broken stumps, brambles, the odd rogue holly tree. Beyond the clearing, the terrain falls off into a two-hundred-yard band of swordferns, hemlocks, cedars, firs, and maples, and far below lies the parking lot for our community's Municipal Hall.

As I dug back into the hillside, I gradually stacked up the retaining wall with rock we'd recently had delivered to build raised beds for the aforementioned organic veggie garden. I'm no engineer—though in Grade 4, a certain engineer did once confine me to my bedroom until I memorized my times tables— which is how I could calculate that 2,400 gallons of water weighs, let's see, um, just over ten tons. Then there was the Tankosaurus itself. Empty, it weighs roughly 250 pounds. By my clueless and wholly unqualified calculations, the cistern would transfer its ten-ton load mostly down into the earth it sits on, but partly out to the sides, which is why the rock wall I built to keep that earth in place would need to be worthy of the task.

Luckily, my terrace-in-progress lies downhill from my rock pile. With the help of my moving dolly, a long steel pry bar, gravity, and my—ahem—wicked Tae Kwon Do–honed quads, I wrestled, over the course of the day, a dozen or so blocky, near-picnic-cooler-sized boulders into place to build up the wall that would retain my tank parking space. It was a task best handled by machine, but access was impossible (my house was in the way). By mid-afternoon, I was ready to receive last rites, but the job was done. The terrace was finished, and it looked reasonably bomber. I tamped the earth with a post and my own work boots—knowing full well I should really be pounding it with a rented tamping machine, but whatever—and began leaving voice mails around the island to address Phase II of the project.

"Hey, Stu, it's James. Hey, I was wondering if you're around tomorrow to help me out with a little favor. I've got this water tank over here that I need to move. It's a little on the awkward side, and we've got to figure out how to get it down a bit of a sketchy slope, so I'm throwing muscle at the problem and lining up about six guys. Can you pitch in for an hour or so? Could really use your help. I'll cue up some cold ones for after we're done. Give me a call. Thanks, man."

My faithful buddy Stu the shipping executive was the first to sign up. He was joined by Richard the Mountie, Greg the management consultant, Brad the middle-school teacher, and Peter the financial adviser. Everyone else, it seemed, had something better to do with their Sunday afternoon than risk his life under the downhill side of a 250-pound plastic tank, poised at the brink of a forty-five-degree slope of loose shale in the drizzling rain. Can you imagine?

Using a set of two-by-four studs as rails, we slid the tank to the brink of the precipice and down onto a small level terrace at the top of the talus slope; the little dirt platform would soon be a kitchen garden, planted with veggies we'd started from seed a month or so back. From there, we'd need to nudge the Tankosaurus about six feet downhill and then somehow slide or roll it horizontally along the slope to the new home I'd carved out for it under the deck, where it would remain more or less forever.

The tank was very heavy, and there was nothing to grab on to. We needed a plan. We needed to MacGyver something together.

"Well, gentlemen, how are we going to go about this?"

Six privately terrified males stared at the Tankosaurus. Our task was ludicrous; peer pressure alone kept us rooted to the spot. If we couldn't keep hold of the thing and it got away from us, it would first flatten whichever unfortunate bastard was standing below it, then crash and bounce down the talus slope. From there, I imagined it picking up speed through the woods until it finally lumbered out of the bush in a puzzling green plastic whirl only to crush Mayor Bob's Toyota Corolla, which I could only assume was parked out of view in the lot below.

"Really, we need something to lower it down the slope here," suggested Stu. "Something we can get the bottom edge of it onto, like a long piece of lumber, a piece of scaffolding, or something."

"Right," concurred Richard the Mountie. "Then we'll be able to roll it along that until we can slide it onto the terrace."

The slope was about twenty-five feet across. On one side lay a sturdy boulder that could anchor a board, on the other, home plate. Publicly, we were pleased with the plan. Privately, each of us was crapping his pants.

"Have you got something that can span this?" asked our law-enforcement representative.

He and I scoured a nearby building site and found a twenty-foot aluminum extension ladder, which we commandeered without asking in the name of conserving our precious island water resources and furthering the cause of food security. The ladder spanned our loose slope in a rickety, dubious arrangement. It looked like some wildly improbable fire-truck rescue scenario that Duncan might have me draw with a crayon. Six quietly terrified males stared down at the ladder, the best arrangement we could come up with. A crane would really have been ideal, or at the very least, one or two more beefy dudes. I'd voice-mailed Dan Parke, but he hadn't yet responded; wisely, he was probably out swimming in his marvelously dated neon-hued wetsuit. I couldn't blame him. Parke would risk more than just his neck out here on the talus slope; if his professional licensing board found out he had a role in such a plainly dangerous six-stooges commando operation, well, let's just say my Eco-Shed might turn out to be *his* last hurrah.

One final piece of Operation Tankosarus had yet to be resolved: we needed to somehow lasso the cistern with a rope. Once we anchored the thing off, we'd theoretically be able to lower it down the embankment to the ladder a few inches at a time, then roll or slide it sideways into its waiting slot. One hitch: The tank is smooth all the way around; there was no molded hook or eye that we might lash a rope to.

I fastened together a pair of two-by-six studs in an X, removed the cap from the access hole in the top of the tank, tucked my studs inside, then tied the rope to them. Our improvised anchor was the very definition of a jerry-rigged, half-assed arrangement, and it was all that would prevent $1,700 worth of green plastic from careening downhill and quite messily flattening anything in its path. But nobody had a better idea.

We needed to loop the other end of the rope around something substantial at the top of the slope—something that would allow us to anchor off the Tankosaurus and permit one of us to lower it downhill onto the ladder an inch at a time.

Nothing presented itself. There was a fence post in the ground nearby, but it was way too flimsy. Then Greg spied our salvation.

"What about your suv? Can you back it up to the edge?"

I could. I'm not sure if Operation Tankosaurus qualified as either "sport" or "utility"—it was probably a little of both—but Padre's hand-me-down luxury rig, the object of my continuing guilt and derision, was just the ticket. I can say with some certainty that no one has ever used a Premium Edition Lexus RX300 to belay a 250-pound plastic cistern, but this green building thing is all about out-of-the-box thinking, *n'est-ce pas?*

I put the trailer hitch into its receiver and backed the Lexus up to the brink of the cliff. If this whole escapade weren't so plainly bizarre and dangerous, it would almost be the kind of thing you could imagine an advertising director latching on to. Either that, or some kind of reality-show stunt aimed at Gen-Y types. We'd all be sporting branded caps (GreenTeam xTreme!), chest-mounted cameras, headsets, and the like. Can't you just picture the circling helicopter shot?

I volunteered to take the downslope side. Richard's wife, Carrie, had shown up to belay with the rope wrapped around the hitch.

"Everybody ready?" financial planner Peter called out. "OK, we're going to nudge it off the edge."

I stood on the slope just down below, ready to guide Tankosaurus down the hill. Yeah, as if I'd be able to do anything other than briefly cry out before sustaining massive internal injuries.

I was expecting the boys to just nudge it forward an inch at a time. But the crew was too enthusiastic. Their first shove took it a good two feet into space over the edge and almost threw me backwards down the slope and into the land of jagged stumps.

"Whoa! Whoa! Stop! Guys! Guys! A little more slowly, please!"

Gently, gradually, Tankosaurus came over the edge. Its lower rim contacted the talus, scraped and bumped downhill for a few anxious moments as I called out its progress, until plastic finally contacted aluminum.

"OK, we're on the ladder! Hold it there!"

The heli-cam zooms in tight on the scene: six people surround an enormous green marshmallow—hey, it could be plastered with sponsors' logos!—balanced perilously on the brink of a drop-off and tied off the hitch of a big-ass luxury suv. A heart-pounding drum track plays over the footage—the remotely amplified cacophony of my heart, which thumps in my chest like a Grateful Dead drum circle on the beach in Sausalito.

Then, disaster!

Just kidding. The operation went so smoothly from there that it was almost as if a network television director had stage-managed the whole thing. Like clockwork, the money guy, the Mountie, the shipping exec, the consultant, the teacher, and the writer carefully scooted Tankosaurus along the aluminum ladder on its bottom edge: the whole thing tipped crazily uphill. After a few tense moments, the team got the leading edge onto the terrace, and with some choreographed effort from six very manly men—every one of whom would doubtless get lucky that night after recounting the tale—the tank landed home.

In the saga of the Eco-Shed, it was truly an epic chapter. All that remained was to lay some pipe in a trench along the foundation leading from the Eco-Shed downspout, under the deck, and into the tank. I'd then install my pump, run a new circuit for it, and plumb a pipe back uphill to the garden. From there, the water would ultimately feed into a spider web of drip-irrigation lines. Chard, carrots, lettuce, beets, blueberries, and apple trees would thrive. And Mother Gaia would move three centimeters closer into balance.

But really, Operation Tankosaurus wouldn't have been the same without Lexus on the team. Oh, sure, maybe Greg could have driven his rig over, but there was something serendipitous and deliciously poetic about the whole episode. The wheels I'd long struggled to distance myself from, my rolling icon of pointless excess, proved useful for more than beach vacation runs. The beast actually played a leading role in the master plan for ecologically upgrading our lives and landscape. It was as if Lexus and I had made our peace. There were no hard feelings. It was all very reasonable and decent.

But I still intended to dump her ass.

10

Fully Loaded

"It'll be so great to see you guys again, Padre. It's been such a long time."

Indeed it had. It was early August. The Eco-Shed was framed and roofed, and the plumbing and ventilation systems were roughed in, which is to say, water, waste, and ventilation pipes and ducts now snaked through walls and ceilings. The electrician had been bumping me off his schedule for a full month while he chased more lucrative projects, and the specialty fiberglass windows were almost ready to ship from eastern Canada.

I was washing the dishes while Elle chatted on the phone with her dad, who said he was planning to come up and visit in a month or so. I could only catch one side of the call, but what I could hear put a small knot in my stomach.

"The studio? Oh it's going really well. It's taking us longer than we figured, though."

[pause]

"Well, it's partly the subtrades. They are all super busy, working on these mansions going up all over the island. You know, a small project like ours is barely worth getting out of bed for. So they fit us in between these other jobs."

[pause]

"Well, we are waiting on the electrical—that's the big hold-up right now—and the windows, too."

[pause]

"Oh, about $75,000, and James thinks he's going to go over about fifteen or twenty K."

[pause]

"Yeah, that's true, but there's a lot of fancy engineering going on in there. You'll see when you come up."

[pause]

"Wow! That would be sweet of you, Padre. I'll try to find out."

Elle hung up and said to me, "My dad just asked me how much it would cost him if he enclosed the carport and turned it into a garage."

"Oh, he did?"

Ah, yes, the carport. The one that no longer exists. I'd only spoken with Padre once or twice since that heady morning I took the controls of the Volvo EC210 excavator. I hadn't yet raised the issue of the carport—it just felt like too much information. But I did mention in one phone call that we were putting the Lexus on the market.

"It's such a nice car, but we can't afford the gas," I told him. "It's costing us seventy dollars to fill the tank these days, and the car burns through it quickly."

After a pause—I think he felt bad for giving us something that ended up stretching our budget—Padre asked me what we were thinking of replacing it with.

"We'd like to get a hybrid, but we can't quite afford one, so we'll probably buy one of those smaller new cars, one of those peppy runabouts, like a Honda Fit or a Toyota Yaris."

Doubtless thinking that this would be pure madness for a young family, he tried to upsell me. "What about a minivan? I hear those are pretty good."

"Yeah, you *can* get a lot of stuff in a van. But we really want to put gas mileage at the top of our shopping list. We'll get something we can put a roof box on for extra cargo when we need it. Maybe get a compact trailer. Lots of people do that in Europe, you know."

Somehow it just did not come up in that conversation—or the one or two that followed—that the new car that would replace the Lexus would be fully exposed to the Canadian elements this winter because there would be no Padre-financed carport sheltering it. Padre didn't yet know this, and the longer I took to tell him, the worse we'd both feel when he found out.

While I didn't exactly take my decision to demoli—uh, "deconstruct"—the thing lightly, I always knew it could result in some familial fallout. Padre means well, but he has a habit of offering us stuff, like carports and luxury SUVs, that are extraordinarily generous but not always our bag. What can we do? A shiny car for Christmas? Hel-lo!? You'd have to be a dummkopf to turn it down. Padre loves us and likes to show it by helping us out the best way he can think of—with gifts that many people would clip off their pinkie to be lucky enough to receive. Thing is, our agendas have about as much in common as the blue states do with the red.

My plan had been to soften any potential negative reaction to the unauthorized carportectomy with the overwhelming coolness of the completed Eco-Shed that would stand in its place. So far, I'd lucked out. Padre and his wife—Elle's stepmom, Cheryl—usually pop up from California for a visit every four or six months. When they had last come by, everything was as it had been since the day we moved in: There was a carport and a studio slab awaiting a small building of vague description.

"So you really think we should tell your dad what we've done up here? You don't want to wait until he gets here and sees it for himself?"

"I don't think that's a good idea, do you?" my loving wife replied. "I think you need to come out and tell him that you demolished his seventeen-thousand-dollar carport."

"Point of clarification. First of all, it wasn't 'his' carport, it was ours, he gave it to us ..."

"You *know* it's more complic ..."

"And second, we didn't *demolish* it. Technically, we *deconstructed* it. Besides, what would be the sense of upsetting him on the phone? I mean, it's difficult to describe what the Eco-Shed is without seeing it and learning how it works. He might not appreciate the full picture if I tell him about it on the telephone, especially if I start babbling about thermal mass and ventilation systems. All he's going to hear is 'carport' and 'gone.'"

Actually, although Padre still doesn't believe human activities are driving global warming—and I wasn't even going to broach the subject of peak oil with him—he does know something about green building. Last fall, in a move that still baffles me, he bought into a brand new sustainably designed resort community, with ambitious plans for renewable energy, rainwater harvesting, and all the rest. He forwards me the occasional shareholders' update e-mail from the developer, whose green creds are absolutely sterling. The missives land in my box right alongside his occasional Newt Gingrich YouTube speech or photo gallery of female cyclists in San Francisco wearing nothing but body paint. I suspect he is plowing some of his green into green not because he's concerned about the fate of the Earth but rather because he's noted the meteoric growth of sustainability—he once bleemed me a green-building article scanned out of *The Robb Report*—and sees it for what it is, a promising investment. He's a savvy real estate developer with a good nose for opportunity.

"I just can't get a read on how he's going to respond," I told my wife.

"That's why you should tell him now. One of these days, he's going to show up, out of the blue—remember how I told you he just appeared that time on my doorstop in Hamburg? I'm worried he might be hurt if you don't give him the courtesy of telling him what you've done."

"Point of clarification: what *we've* done."

"Huh."

"You think I should call him? What would I say?"

"Here," Elle said, "I'm my dad, and you're you. Go."

"Hey, Padre, it's your deadbeat son-in-law. How are you doing? What are you up to?"

"Oh, we're doing great," Elle replied. "We went to a golf tournament last week with Pat and Bob out in Palm Desert."

"Oh, that sounds awesome. Hope the weather was good for you. Say, Padre, there's something I've been meaning to tell you—it's a little awkward."

"Oh yeah, what's that?"

"I'm gay."

"Very funny."

"All right. You know how I've been building the studio next to the house? You know how it's going to be a supergreen building and all, like that development you bought into last year? Part of the deal is it's specially designed to be heated in the winter by the sun, but to do that we needed southern exposure to make the thing work ..."

"Uh-huh."

"The carport was blocking the sun, so we kind of had to ... dismantle it."

"Wait, what do you mean you 'dismantled' it? But you're putting it back together some place else, right?"

"Not exactly. It was so nice of you to build it for us, and we got a couple of good years of use out of it, but we couldn't find another way around it. So we sold the timbers and took up the concrete."

"It's gone?"

"It's gone."

"When did this happen?"

"A few months ago. Back in the spring. Are you mad?"

"No, I'm not mad. I'm glad you told me."

"Me, too," I replied.

"Not bad," said Elle. "I would maybe spend more time on the chitchat at the front end, though, but I think you should just come out with it. Just like that."

"Should I call him now, while it's fresh in my memory?" I asked Elle.

"Nah, not tonight. But call him soon."

※ ※ ※

The Web is the world's most accurate appraisal device. When it comes to finding something's market value down to the dime, the network is brutally honest and ruthlessly efficient. I know this, because for four months I had been trying, and failing, to sell my Lexus RX 300 luxury SUV on Craigslist, the ultimate Wild West semi-underground digital bazaar.

In May, I'd optimistically listed the rig at $23,999. Not a single e-mail crossed my desk, so I knocked $500 off the price. A few nibbles, but still no serious buyers. I got a guy with a significant language barrier and a scammer who promised—for a "fully refundable" up-front three-hundred-dollar retainer—that he'd deliver me a buyer within six weeks. I posted a few more nice photos and knocked off another five hundred dollars. Still nothing. Another five hundred dollars down, a few better photos, and a tweak of the ad copy. The response remained underwhelming; buyers weren't exactly breaking down my door.

I reluctantly dropped the price below twenty thousand dollars, a dangerous threshold for me because it approximated the price of the zippy ultraefficient replacement vehicle we'd set our sights on. (At about thirty-four grand, including taxes, a hybrid remained far out of reach.) Any lower than twenty K, and we'd start putting money on the table to swap out the vehicle. Given the Eco-Shed debt we were already servicing—as expected, the studio was proving a rather expensive experiment—we didn't want to do that. We wanted to reduce our transportation foot-print, but not if it meant piling on more debt to do it. We were already into this greener life way over our heads.

Elle reread my ad copy. "This is too quiet," she declared. "Sex it up! Start frickin' *selling* this thing. Connect with the target market. Think about it: Who really wants this car, and what would tickle their soft spot?"

Recalling my surreal visit to the dealership, I imagined a young, on-the-make broker type, someone who flogs hedge funds all day—whatever *those* are—then books it for the slopes every other weekend. And so while Elle kicked back in front of the TV, as long-haul commuters do, I dropped the price to nine-teen thousand dollars and rewrote the ad. The new copy stressed adventure with cash and read in part as follows:

Whistler? Tons of cargo room, heated seats, 230-watt Nakamichi six-CD seven-speaker sound system, 60/40 folding rear seats for clubs or ski/board gear, and "snow mode" traction switch make this one a sweet pick for Sea-to-Sky runs. Plus sport racks up top!

Creature comforts? Buttery tan leather interior, one-touch seat memory, power-adjustable seats, heated mirrors, heated front seats. The brand is the mark of quality, inside and out.

Passing power? A 3.0-Liter 220hp four cam 24-Valve V6 engine responds when you need it to!

The classified made no mention of glitchy instrument display screens. "Now you're talkin'—that's much better," said Elle, previewing the creative. "See, you *are* a salesman. That should hook you a few buyers."

It hooked me one. I took the Lexus downtown to meet up with David, a nice boomer who'd worked for decades as a hospital electrician. He was a little flustered behind the wheel—as if he were driving something a bit too blue blood for him—and kept asking how much the maintenance would cost and how expensive the parts would be if something broke. The Lexus was clearly just out of his league. But then he mentioned something that gave me a clue about why prospects weren't beating down my door.

"Part of the problem is that it's an American car," he said. "And that's going to make it harder for me to resell if I want to later."

"Why is that important?" I asked. "I mean, it's exactly the same car you'd buy in Canada, only with a different speedometer, right?"

"Actually, there've been a lot of problems with people bringing cars up from the States that have been in floods and bad stuff like that."

Uh oh.

After a couple of months of aggressive online marketing, the Lexus was still sitting on Lot 55, and part of the reason had nothing to do with fuel economy. In the eyes of potential buyers, my fully loaded rig was of questionable geographic origin.

I had imported Padre's rolling palace when we moved up from Santa Fe a couple years back. It easily passed muster with the Canadian authorities. But that wasn't good enough for my gun-shy prospects. In recent years, a number of my fellow countrymen had found themselves bilked into buying U.S. cars that had ridden out a variety of natural disasters. A few scammers sneaked a truckload or two of these write-offs across the border and passed them off as nearly new, functioning vehicles.

In one widely circulated horror story, one poor bastard only realized his new car was not as it seemed when he took its malfunctioning CD player into a shop. When the techs opened it up, they noticed something unusual: The stereo was full of sand. Everything in the car quickly went south from there, in the footsteps of the seller, who vanished back into the land of opportunity and was never seen again.

Around these parts, any auto with miles on the speedometer instead of kilometers is considered a potential FEMA case and treated accordingly. You can't blame people, really. I'd probably feel the same way. After hemming and hawing for a couple days, the hospital worker called me back. "It's a really nice vehicle, but we think this is just too much car for us."

Of course, the wheel rims weren't helping our case. The day Padre signed the car over to us, the chrome finish began flaking off them like the fourth day of a bad sunburn. The corroded rims issue is a manufacturer's defect, a common gripe well documented in Lexus chat groups. The problem is purely cosmetic; it has nothing to do with salty roads or, God forbid, driving in the surf, but it turns buyers off. Nothing says "storm surge" quite like a set of scabby wheels. We could replace them to improve our vehicle's marketability, but a new set would cost us, at minimum, fifteen hundred dollars. *Ka-ching*. And unfortunately, the vehicle also needed new tires and brakes. *Ka-ching, ka-ching*.

Reducing our transportation footprint was proving to be more complicated than we'd ever imagined. Taking care of all these maintenance items would bring our profit down well below the sticker price of the gas-sipper car we'd set our sights on—especially since American vehicles sell well below market value in Canada anyway. We'd end up greening our lives the same way we were doing with the Eco-Shed: on credit. It could be the breaking point, the first step toward the inevitable conclusion: *foreclosure, divorce, messy custody battle . . .*!

The unimpressed hospital electrician proved to be just the first in a series of time-wasting appointments that went nowhere. A chubby mid-fifties Russian fellow came over to Bowen to kick the fast-balding tires. He knew our SUV needed a little maintenance work, but the price was right. He took it for a spin and—even though our kids had long since nullified the $289.95 detailing job—he pronounced it very nice. "Except for the wheels."

"Yeah, I don't know why they're flaking like that," I said. (I hadn't yet googled the issue.) "But the car is otherwise in perfect shape."

"There's only one reason I can think of why the finish would be coming off," he replied. "It's been in salt water. Did you live close to the ocean?"

"No, we lived in the desert, and they don't salt the roads in New Mexico, either."

"Well, if it was in any water, my mechanic would see corrosion on the undercarriage."

"That's fine—he won't find any," I snipped. "This car has never been near the water."

"I believe you," he said. "You seem honest."

I was. Mostly. I didn't mention the display-screen hiccup from that so-called last road trip some months back. I kept telling myself it was an isolated incident; the dealer went over the electrical system with fancy Lexus sensors and probes and gave it a clean bill of health. There's nothing wrong with this car, I'd assured myself.

I'm one of those people who, when pulled over by a cop, starts babbling confessions to crimes I have never committed. A part of me secretly believed this honest deal was really a scam. And I'm a pathetic liar. I knew how it would play out. The Russian would sit in the front seat and pop open the glove box. And a putrid fish would flop out and land in his lap.

"I'll think about it, and I'll e-mail you," he said. It was the last I heard from him.

* * *

By this point, my marriage was really beginning to feel the strain. The Eco-Shed was more than six months behind schedule and was looking to come in about twenty-five K over budget—mostly because of wildly unrealistic ballpark cost estimates on a variety of line items, including insulation, windows, and labor needed to reclaim the reclaimed wood. By this point I was just over a year—and sixty-five thousand dollars—in over my head on my way up to a revised final projected tab of a cool eighty-nine thousand bills. We were still waiting for windows that hadn't arrived. And trying to sell a high-end American SUV was proving to be nothing short of an ordeal.

Careerwise, I was in a slump. Even as I spent money hand over fist in the front yard, try as I might, I was just not bringing in my share of the monthly household income. My official excuse? To an editor who might give me work, I was as geographically undesirable as the RX 300 still parked out in my driveway. I was the very definition of "out of the loop."

For magazine writers, original ideas are everything. You glean them from a network of sources and contacts, keeping the connections well lubricated with regular drinks, coffees, receptions, junkets, and trade shows. But I'd spent most of the past year out of circulation in a basement on a small island in the middle of a fjord. Instead of touching base, checking in, doing lunch, catching up, I'd been assembling complicated German toys with tiny plastic screwdrivers. For me, working the room meant hoovering up the dust bunnies under the couch.

Although I thrive on forward motion, the Eco-Shed project was stalled like a Parish County Pacer. Meanwhile, the stress was simmering away, approaching a slow boil. "We really need you to hit your monthly minimum," Elle reminded me one evening, her lips pursed.

There were a number of big to-dos remaining on my Type A checklist: Finish the stupid Eco-Shed. Sell the stupid car. Finish the next stupid assignment. Then, perhaps, get a stupid job. Forge ahead with my freshly greened, theoretically happier, carbon-reduced life. And of these action items, number two—get rid of Padre's vehicular gift—was starting to feel like a chain around my neck. Elle and I knew we could walk into a dealer and trade in our wheels for a new, über-efficient car any time, but we also knew that said dealer would take us to the cleaners. Going this easy route would mean signing up for a new monthly payment that we couldn't absorb.

We could also buy a used car off Craigslist—an older, smaller vehicle, perhaps a Toyota or Honda. The more sanctimonious greens love to crow about the energy and emissions that go into manufacturing a new vehicle. An older, smaller car would go much farther on a tankful than we do now, yes. But we wanted near-hybrid efficiency. And, as you may have gathered by now, we were done with compromises. If Elle and I ever organized a symposium of stubborn sons-of-bitches, we wouldn't even bother inviting anyone else.

But sheer obstinacy wasn't solving this puzzle. "The way I see it, we've got to make a choice—*now*," said my frazzled wife. She'd just checked the bank accounts on the laptop; our mortgage had just been pulled, plus the latest Eco-Shed payment, leaving us with around two hundred dollars until Elle's next payday—in, um, two weeks.

"The thing isn't selling, you're taking it to the city to show it to people who aren't buying it—wasting time that you don't have. They're not buying it because of the rims, which we don't want to sink thousands into replacing. And besides, you should be using your day care days to hustle up some work, not play salesman. This whole thing is turning into a theater of the absurd," she frothed.

"I know; I feel like we've got way, way too much going on."

"We either slash the price and just unload the thing and finance something else, or we keep it forever and just be happy with that. End of story."

That night, I signed on to Craigslist and rolled back the price, Wal-Mart-style, down to eighteen thousand dollars. It hurt. That was about five grand less than what used-car dealers were asking for Canadian versions of the same make, model, year, and mileage. And ding, just like that, I cottoned on to my customer.

Gary and Donna were a couple from the 'burbs who were cruising into the empty-nester years. They'd been driving their worn Toyota Previa minivan since the kids were at soccer camp. After decades of delayed gratification, during which they forked out cash for piano lessons, calculus textbooks, braces, summer camp, and so on, they were ready to treat themselves to something special—something with heated leather seats, power lumbar support, and six-speaker Nakamichi sound.

All this time, my online pitch had been targeting the wrong customer. I was not after the young on-the-make Whistler-phile trying to impress the new client. That guy is out financing the brand new Lexus that parks itself on command. Or even worse, he's throwing it down for the new Lexus RX 400H, the first luxury hybrid SUV. Mr. Whistler, I realized, would feel as if he were lowering his standards to buy our (used and flaking) wheels. I needed a prospect who felt as though he were *raising* them. I needed an aspirational Lexus driver.

Hello, Gary. He took the car for a spin with his wife, Donna. We haggled a bit and settled on a price that reflects the money he would need to put into brakes and tires: $17,250. The deal looked done; he even had a bank draft drawn up in my name. All that was needed was an inspection and a signature. With the end of the saga in sight, I blew another precious day care morning while a mainland mechanic gave it the once-over. A day or so later, Gary called back.

"I just heard back on the inspection, and I'm afraid I didn't hear what I was expecting to hear."

Gulp.

"To be honest, James, he says he can't recommend the car."

I flash to an image of a grease monkey extracting a tangle of Gulf Coast seaweed from my engine compartment.

"Why on earth not?"

"Well, it's a number of things. He says the timing belt hasn't been replaced. He says there's a dent in a rocker panel underneath where someone raised the car and didn't put the jack in the right place. He says there is a leaking seal on the front axle."

Timing belt? Rocker panel? *Leaking axle seal?* How come my mechanic hadn't mentioned any of this?

"Gary, I'm stunned. I had no idea any of this was going on."

"I know that, and I feel bad, but we're feeling a little spooked."

"It sounds like the deal is off then."

"Yes, at this point, it looks that way."

I was crushed. We were *this close!*

It was time to bite the bullet and dump some money into the car. The next day, I ordered four new tires ($703.96) and took the car to Chris Leigh, my island mechanic, who replaced the timing belt and brakes ($1,036.54). He couldn't find anything wrong with the axle. "It's sweating a tiny bit," Leigh said of the gasket in question, "but I'd consider that a normal condition. In my opinion, it doesn't need replacing."

I called Gary back and rambled into his voice mail: I've replaced the timing belt, tires, and brakes, I told him. I assured him the seal was fine. I asked him if he still wanted the car for eighteen thousand dollars. After a while, he called back. He said he'd think it over.

The prospect who went so far as to cut a bank draft in my name considered my new offer, then e-mailed me a few days later: "We've decided to not to purchase another vehicle for a while. We'll carry on with the Previa. Good luck."

Gary's kiss-off turned out to be one of three pieces of bad news in a *dies horribilis*. First thing in the morning, in the middle of a phone interview, my computer's hard drive shit the bed, vaporizing two weeks' worth of work. Later in the day, Elle took our neurotic and largely ignored tuxedo cat, Sid, to the vet for a series of booster shots. The moment we brought him home, he began projectile vomiting all over the living room.

Some days are like that. At least nobody we knew was decapitated. We stuck an IV into Sid (OK, so the vet did), dumped the kids into their beds, and promptly downed a bottle of nonlocal cabernet sauvignon. Or two. I can't remember exactly.

Perhaps it was the alcohol in my system, but that night I dreamed of the Eco-Shed. It was quite vivid: Konrad Jaschke, Bowen Island's jolly German building inspector, put a ladder against the side of the studio, climbed up, and held a large carpenter's square against the side of the roof. It wasn't even close to ninety degrees. "Look at zees, James," he called down to me. I did and saw that the Eco-Shed resembled a Dr. Seuss doodle. The whole thing was terrifically askew and not in a groovy Frank Gehry kind of way. Jaschke shrugged. "I'm sorry, zees isn't going to verk. I have to fail zees inspection. I need you to take zee whole seeng down and start over, ya?"

Mercifully, my wife kicked me awake. "You're moaning in your sleep again," she hissed, as my body struggled to process the adrenaline. "For God's sake, I have to be up at five-thirty."

* * *

But just when things seemed at their grimmest, the doom lifted. I posted a new ad, wearily trying to lure my target buyer ("Ready to treat yourself?" the pitch began). Two days later, I was putting away laundry. Sabrina was in the tub, and her brother was cued up to take her place, when the phone rang. I flopped down on the bed to answer it. It was my dad. He'd been following the Lexus saga closely. The previous day I'd told him about the *dies horribilis.*

"I was just looking at your ad on Craigslist this morning," he said.

"Yeah?"

"Your mum and I have just had a long conversation, and if it's all right with you, we'd like to buy the Lexus."

My jaw hit the floor, bounced twice, and rolled under the dresser.

Permit me to freeze the footage for a moment here and explain why Dad's statement makes about as much sense as a ripe papaya in Nunavut. British immigrants to Canada in the early 1960s, my parents are shining examples of what the Protestant work ethic can accomplish. My father was a teacher who worked at the same institute of technology for thirty-five years; my mum—a nurse for ten years—raised three children. The two of them are greener than I'll ever be, because they seem to operate quite comfortably without buying much of anything other than mostly generic groceries. My dad repairs things—Sabrina's wind-up music box, for example—that most of us would simply throw out. They are thrifty to the point of self-deprivation. But as a result, they are now living the retirement those mutual-fund companies are forever pitching me. With a mega-mortgage and two kids in child care, Elle and I are hopelessly behind on our retirement savings. We feel as if we're in survival mode, and my pricey green larks aren't yet generating the promised dividends of happiness.

Meanwhile, my dad is Mr. Chipper. He gets a kick out of saving a few cents at the pump. Some people get a little *frisson* out of a bargain; to my professional engineer father, it's more about beating the system. To him, the marketplace is a puzzle to be cracked. Here is a man who gleefully squeezes every possible nickel out of a deal, a guy who never pays full retail, who was into eBay and Craigslist long before they even existed. When I was a kid, he would scoop up ski equipment at church rummage sales for next to nothing, then flip the gear through the free-ad papers. In one of my most vivid childhood memories, a whole family showed up and tried on ski boots in the front hall. They left fully geared up for the slopes, my dad grinning with a roll of bills in his pocket.

Then there was the Great Vacuum Tube Initiative. Sometime in the early 1980s, my father caught wind of an electronics distributor liquidating its inventory. To my mother's abject horror, he snapped up the company's stock—which consisted of hundreds and hundreds of mostly obsolete glass tubes that powered oscilloscopes, high-fi amps, television sets, and the like. Dad stacked flats of them in the nicest room in the house, a space with a patio outside and a panoramic view, originally built as a parental retreat for him and Mum.

This was not as bizarre a move as we all at first believed; the tubes were indeed headed for the technology scrap pile. But this was an era in which you could not only build your own home electronics, but you could actually *repair them when they broke*. Dad had calculated that a sizable population of hobbyist audiophiles would still need a fresh tube now and again to keep their Marshall guitar amps humming.

He put an ad in the classifieds and waited for customers. Every so often, a call would come in.

"Hi there. Yes, I still have some tubes. An AE35? Hmmm, I think I've got a few of those; let me check the list."

He'd rummage through his inventory. "Yes, it looks as though I've got three. How many do you need?" And just like that, one phone call at a time, he gradually paid off his investment and cleared a small profit. It literally took years to flip those tubes. He didn't mind. All he needed was warehouse space, and he had that. Sort of.

Then, more recently, there was the Free Breakfast Incident. It was late 2003, and Elle and I were living in Santa Fe. Sabrina was a toddler, and Duncan was just a few months old. Mum and Dad had flown down to visit—on points, of course—to see the new baby. To stay out of our hair, they'd booked into a nearby motel that offered a seniors' discount. We only had a few days together, so we wanted to make the most of the visit.

"Why don't you come over for breakfast—I'll make pancakes," Elle suggested on the phone the night they arrived. "We'll whip up a stack with strawberries, some fresh OJ, some nice tea."

There was an uncomfortable silence on the other end of the line.

"Well, normally we'd be delighted," my dad replied. "But you see, our hotel offers a free breakfast with the room. It would be a shame to pass that up; we wouldn't be getting our full value out of the deal."

I could go on, but you get the idea. A part of me deeply admires my dad's relentless thrift, self-reliance, and resourcefulness. On that same trip, noticing that our doorbell was broken, Dad opened his suitcase and—incredibly—produced a small voltage tester, which he used to diagnose and repair the chime. (How about a show of hands: does anyone else out there bring a *pocket voltmeter* along on vacation? I didn't think so.) But although memories like this fill me with pride, another side of me just wants to hit Starbucks once in a while for a grande latte—even though *yes, I can make a coffee at home!*

That is why the Lexus is the last car in the world I could imagine my parents wanting or driving. Up until now, they'd driven a 1988 Nissan Stanza.

I found my words at last. "Are you joking?"

"We're quite serious. We've got company coming from England for a few weeks this fall, and we'll need lots of space. And besides, we decided that it's something we're ready for. We think it will be lots of fun. We'll pay your full asking price, of course."

Part of his offer is clearly filial aid—Mum and Dad want to support us and help underwrite our almost-green life. But it's not an entirely selfless move, either. After decades of putting their splurges on hold, they're ready to treat themselves. A long-estranged relative has recently been diagnosed with bone cancer. Mum and Dad are doubtless grappling with their own mortality. They are Gary and Donna, twenty years later. After a life of "Let's book that window cabin next summer," with four grandchildren swarming around them, my parents are ready to toss caution to the wind. The car that to us feels like a symbol of planetary overshoot is to them a yummy indulgence. Like the Häagen-Dazs ice cream they savored for the first time at our house—"This really is quite good!" Mum declared—the Lexus is the forbidden fruit they are now ready to bite into.

There are other reasons to feel good that the RX 300 has found a home in my dad's suburban driveway. Mum isn't as mobile as she once was, and the Lexus will be far easier for her to get in and out of. My conscience on the fritzy display will be clear—Dad has listened to my hand-wringing for months. Best of all, my parents barely drive at all. If our seventeen-mile-per-gallon vehicle is to land in a new driveway, it should be Dad's, where it will go to the mall now and then, but not much farther. The car will remain in the family, transferred from one in law to another, with a few years of child-schlepping duty in between. Every so often, the Lexus will come over and visit and touch bumpers with the zippy Honda Fit that will replace it. The luxury vehicle will be deeply appreciated and respected, and isn't that all any of us wants?

Then again, who am I kidding? Can someone out there please reach over and slap me? Because my endless neurotic hand-wringing and eco-guilt processing has again overshadowed a greater simpler truth: My 'rents bailed us out, plain and simple. They took the thing off our hands because that's what mums and dads do, and mine do it particularly well.

Then I remember the dealer's Web site. Man, they really bungled it. The Lexus RX 300 definitely *is* my father's car.

11

Reality Check

The opening scene of my worst nightmare begins late in the afternoon on a hypothetical Thanksgiving Day, about a decade out into the future. In my dream, a storm is roaring across the hillside and buffeting our cozy home. Standing at the living room window, I take in the line of striking white windmills up along the ridge of Mount Collins, silently cranking out what I imagine will be some of Howe Sound's finest carbon-free juice.

As the sequence begins, I joke with Elle that we're using more than our fair share of that precious power. The kids are now teenagers, and they're upstairs getting ready for a holiday dinner in the way that adolescents have done since the invention of alternating current. Sabrina, for example, is taking the world's longest shower, pulling 120 precious amps out of the island's grid every moment. The bathroom fans are clearing steam, the clothes dryer is finishing the laundry. But as is typical of my tomorrow-dreams, there are a few William Gibsonesque twists:

Duncan is up in his room "prescencing" in Vienna with Carmen, his latest girlfriend.

But it's not all sci-fi: A nice bed of coals is glowing in the woodstove, while a turkey finishes in the oven alongside carrots, turnips, parsnips, and beets that I pulled from our own soil earlier that day. The house swirls with delicious aromas. I can almost smell them in my sleep.

I flop down on the couch in front of the wood stove, waiting for some strange herbal concoction to clear up a mild headache that's been nagging at me—the only thing putting a damper on the afternoon. Elle is in the kitchen basting our giant roasting bird, which in this protein-constrained, post-suv fantasy future is evidently a rare treat, indeed.

"Oh hell, I've spilled fat on the burner," my wife says, turning the range-hood fan up to its highest setting to vent the smoke.

"Don't worry about it, it'll clear in a moment." As she fusses with side dishes and plates, I stretch out on the couch. Still lots of time. The headache is gone, but I'm still feeling under the weather. Must be coming down with something.

"I think these deadlines are catching up to me," I say as I curl up with the blanket. "Have I only had that one glass of mead? I feel like I could go to sleep right now." In reply, she drops a pan of the veggies on the kitchen floor with a large crash. "Shit!"

That's when the domestic tableau starts to go wrong. I glance over to my wife. She is picking through cupboards. "Where is that dustpan?" she says, pausing to lean on the kitchen island. She opens the fridge and roots around inside. "I know it's around here somewhere." Her words are slurred.

Hmmm, what's she doing looking for a broom in the fridge? That doesn't make sense, does it? Or maybe it does, I can't seem to figure it out. And why do I feel so lethargic?

I am struggling to wake up—both in the dream, and *from* the dream. My eyelids refuse to obey. Whatever, I'll just let Elle get on with it—uh, that thing that she was doing—and snooze here for a bit. She finds the broom and starts cleaning up. Then, after a few minutes, a realization begins to surface from deep in my foggy brain. Something isn't quite right.

"Hon, are you ok?"

She doesn't respond. Still struggling to break free of what I now know is a slow-build deja-vu subconscious horror, I lift my head with what now feels like a Herculean effort, and peer over the back of the couch. My wife is curled up on the kitchen floor alongside the broken dish.

"Sabrina! Duncan!" I mean to yell, but I only mange to utter a drawn-out low-bass noise, like one of my vintage twelve-inch Smiths singles running at sixteen RPM. There's no reply from upstairs. Still locked in the nightmare, I try to drag myself towards my wife. Why aren't my legs working? That's when I salvage what common sense remains in my addled head and put it together.

In the dream I whistle and attract the attention of another Gibsonesque device—this one mounted on the kitchen wall. It looks like some combination of an oversized iPhone and, bizarrely, a 1970s faux-wood-grain home-intercom system, with little levers and buttons. The screen brightens and the unit chirps: "Number please?"

Wait. What was it again?

"Niiinnnee... onnne... onnnne..."

The thingamajig emits a sharp error tone, then responds in a familiar and terrifying monotone: "I'm sorry, James, I can't do that."

As my future self slips unconscious—paralyzed by an odorless and invisible peril that I realize, too late, is flooding my cozy island home—I wake up from my dream in the here and now. And I thank my lucky stars—and a man named Troy Glasner, one of the last green gurus to hop aboard my carousel—that it won't be coming true.

* * *

The Eco-Shed's windows did eventually show up on Lot 55. But not before I lost Jeremy Galpin.

The manufacturer had promised to ship my highly efficient specialty glass on August 5, but because of a glitch at the final assembly stage, the order didn't land on Lot 55 until almost five weeks later—almost three full months after the firm processed my deposit. No amount of calling or e-mailing or swearing or brow-furrowing or cajoling would have hustled the glass through the pipe any faster. Believe me, I tried.

I knew from the beginning that the smaller outfit would take longer to produce the Eco-Shed's windows, but I didn't have a choice. Although the big-name glazing companies can fill orders like a drive-thru crew at McDonald's, their menu is similarly limited. They aren't yet in the business of making super-efficient fiberglass-framed windows with the special low-E hard coat that is designed to admit, not repel, the sun's warmth.

Without that molecules-thick coating, the eighty-odd square feet of glass on my south-facing wall would fend off whatever warming winter rays deigned to land on Bowen Island, instead of inviting them to soak into my expensively insulated, exposed concrete floor. But in the world of windows, mine were still fairly out-there assemblies. This was no fast-food order-by-combo deal. Like so many other things in my Eco-Shed, I would have to wait. And wait some more.

The unexpected delay brought my project to a standstill for the full month of August—which would have been the ideal time to seal the building, insulate, and get the siding on before the first "Pineapple Express" warm fronts arrived from Hawaii, marking the start of six months of torrential rain. If we had had the glass.

Once the glass did arrive, the rest of the project would indeed finish up very quickly, just as Heather Choi had promised almost a year before. But my carpenter won't be the guy to do it. After completing some truly outstanding work, my friend Jeremy Galpin—the original Mr. Good 'Nuff—reluctantly walked away from my Eco-Shed. He'd expected to finish the project by now, but, as feared months ago, the endlessly delayed windows had idled the critical path. Galpin had another job starting up in the Fraser Valley in a week or two, and he couldn't push it back.

"We both knew this was coming," he said, clearly feeling bad for moving on. He offered a few names of guys who might pick up where he left off, but he might as well have promised to find me a hot date at a Yukon mining camp. Blame the pending Winter Olympics, blame Vancouver's notorious livability, blame the city's affluent boomers who were cashing out and building dream homes, but Metro Vancouver remained locked in a roaring construction boom. "I've never seen anything like it in my whole career," confirmed Greg Sims, my heating and ventilation contractor. "Everyone I know has more work than they can handle."

Anyone who could swing a hammer within a hundred miles of Lot 55 was out buying themselves a new pickup truck with cash. According to data compiled by a regional credit union association, in the first half of 2007, building permit values in nearby Vancouver shot up 27 percent over the same period the previous year, to around $4 billion.

I briefly courted a delightful Irish carpenter named Harry who was working on a nearby job site—the same guy who made cracks about landing helicopters on the Eco-Shed's roof—until his boss very politely told me to scram. "We can try and fit you in wherever we can, James," said the man who will keep Harry in Guinness long after my Eco-Shed is finished, "when we have little lulls here and there." We both knew there would be no little lulls until November.

In the meantime, my plumber zoomed through and finished roughing in the Eco-Shed's three-quarter bath and sink fixtures. Then my electrician followed close behind. We'll call him Sparks. His helpers pulled cable through the walls and installed a 200-amp service panel, which is, for a 280-square-foot studio, on the large side. That's because although my lighting and heating systems will all be super-efficient, the Eco-Shed will need a serious shot of juice every time someone turns on a faucet.

Early in the design process, Parke and I had decided to dispense with a hot-water tank in the studio. There's a shower and sink in the space for overnight guests to use, but they won't be used often. It would make little sense to keep a hot-water tank tucked away under the sink, constantly drawing electricity to keep a supply at bathing temperature. Instead, Parke and I specified an on-demand model.

In most cases, this means a small natural gas- or propane-fired unit that heats the water the moment it begins moving in the pipes and vents the combustion gases outside. But I would rather not burn fossil fuels in the Eco-Shed. The solution was an electrically fired on-demand device, which, like so many other things in my studio, is a bit of a rarity—and, at $1,024.22, around five times the price of the conventional tank-style heater it would replace.

And it fairly terrified my man Sparks. "I've got to say, James, the idea of that thing scares the crap out of me," he confided to me in his diluted South African accent when I asked him if he'd install it. Why? Because I'd just told him that the unit in question—it was about the size of a large shoebox and would mount under the sink—draws current through a trio of 40-amp breakers. For those of you who were chewing gum and passing notes in Science 12, that is one a hell of a punch.

I'd rather only pull power out of the grid when needed. That said, when I *do* draw juice, I'll *really* draw it; when someone turns on a hot-water faucet in the Eco-Shed, the flowing water will trip a switch and unleash a tremendous jolt of electricity that will instantly cook the water as it moves through a fine lattice on its way to my sink and showerhead. To get an idea of the amount of current we're talking about, picture three clothes dryers running simultaneously. Indeed, the small box under the Eco-Shed's kitchen sink will pull more than half the total electrical service capacity of my entire house. Which is why Sparks wasn't wild about the idea.

"I'll install it for you if you really want me to," he said. I did, and so he did. To the beats of a rap radio station thumping out of my DeWalt DW911 job-site radio, his crew swept through the place. Within the space of a few hours, they installed switch and light boxes and pulled a spaghetti maze of wires through the walls to connect them. They also installed the #1-gauge cable that would be dedicated to my nearly carbon-neutral on-demand hot-water unit. The wire itself was ridiculously fat; it evoked the terrifying black tentacles on the sentinel robots that patrol the underground world of *The Matrix*.

Meanwhile, as Kanye West and 50 Cent thumped away in the background, my search for a builder continued. The windows were finally on a truck on the other side of the country and were making their way west, and I had no one to install them. I outlined my conundrum to my kind neighbor John Stiver, a professional guitarist, while his son played Captain Blastoff in the backyard with Duncan.

"Did you try Cody Bentall and Tom Taylor?" my neighbor asked. "Those guys built our house. In fact, I think they framed yours. They're really, really good. I'll dig up their numbers for you."

I immediately recalled Bentall from the previous summer, when I'd watched Stiver's house going up just across the cul-de-sac. I also remembered that I had some karmic credit on file with him. In my last days as a contributing editor for a blessedly short-lived guy's gear magazine, I came into some fairly high-end road-bicycle swag, including an ultralightweight helmet, shoes, and shades. Noticing that one of the dudes working next door rode skinny tires up from the ferry dock to the job site each day—a wicked Tour de France–grade climb—I offered him a pair of pricey leftover sunglasses that needed a loving home. I wasn't going to be able to use them, and the unofficial swag code forbade me from Craigslisting the stuff.

"Dude, no way, are you kidding me?" he said as he slipped on the shields with a broad smile. It was a no-brainer for me, but the gesture clearly made his month and imprinted me in his mind.

Now, a year later, the same guy was standing in the framed, plumbed, and wired Eco-Shed, listening to me blather on about passive-solar this and reclaimed that. Everything was ready to go: The windows and front door were sitting right there in an eight-foot-high crate. I'd planed and beveled and stained all the reclaimed-cedar siding that Galpin and I had sourced from Ian Peterson, an enthusiastic salvaged-lumber dealer who keeps a stash of material about an hour's drive deeper into the burbs than Karl Simmerling's operation. This old-growth, clear-grained wood had once stood as pilings in the Fraser River; some of the edge grain even showed evidence of barnacle growth until I ripped it off with a borrowed table saw.

Bentall took it all in: the unusual double north wall, the wood stove, the barnacles. "So what do you think?" I asked him, hopefully. "Do you think you can fit me into a lull somewhere?"

"Tell you what—I'll do better than that. I'll be over with the guys first thing Monday and we'll get you all taken care of," he said.

I felt as if I'd just made a pass at the prom queen, expecting she'd throw her Coke in my face, and in response she'd planted one on me.

"We'll get all this exterior done for you. We'll install the windows, the flashings, trim, and siding. I figure it will take three days or so. That work for you?"

Yeah, I said, feeling waves of relief wash over me. It did.

* * *

With my über-glazing scheduled to go into pre-assigned places in the Eco-Shed, the time had come to line up what may be the studio's second most important ingredient—the material that comes first to mind after windows when we consider where we'll get the biggest bang for our energy buck: insulation.

Although home insulation might well be one of the most boring subjects in the universe, it was a crucial fork in my project's critical path. That's because most houses out there, mine included, leak heat. And they do so because their exterior walls are hurriedly stuffed with batts of fiberglass.

It may not be fair to pick on the fiberglass industry, especially given the hard truths I am about to share about our chosen substitute. And to be fair, fiberglass batts usually include a high proportion of recycled-glass content, and they do a reasonable job of keeping the warmth inside a house when they're installed carefully and under ideal conditions. But in reality, that's hardly ever the case, and because the fluff is quickly covered up by drywall, there's no practical way for a homeowner to tell if it's cut to the right size and if it's where it needs to be. Improperly installed batts can settle in the stud bays, leaving gaps at the tops of walls, and wherever the installer compresses them—for example, to squish the insulation behind a plumbing pipe, wire, or receptacle box—the material's effectiveness plummets. Studies conducted by Oak Ridge National Laboratory in California have found that a standard two-by-six R-19 exterior wall filled with fiberglass batts can actually perform as low as R-11 out in the real world.

Despite fiberglass's dubious effectiveness, there's a very good reason our suburbs are swaddled in acres of the stuff (excellent, you *have* been paying attention): cost. A bundle of batts that will insulate a ten-foot length of two-by-six exterior wall runs about fifty dollars and can be installed for about twenty dollars' worth of labor. The puff-n-stuff meets code and helps keep the initial cost of a home low, but as with electric baseboard heaters, the buyer pays for it in the long run. We all do.

To keep our Eco-Shed's heating costs to a minimum—and our carbon footprint as close to zero as possible—Dan Parke and I employed the principles of passive-solar design. We oriented the building due south and created a thermal mass to absorb and radiate heat. But owing to the scarcity of winter sun on the B.C. coast, we also had an electric-powered hydronic in-floor radiant heat system and a small efficient woodstove as backup. For any of these to operate as hoped—in other words, as infrequently as possible—and maintain our low carbon footprint, we needed a completely sealed, airtight building. And fiberglass just wasn't going to cut it.

Parke and I opted for a "spray-in-place" insulation that would completely fill all the voids between the wall studs and rafters and wouldn't settle, attract bugs, or grow mold. It would dry out on its own if it got wet and, once installed, would emit no harmful volatile organic compounds (vocs) or toxic substances. Many options fit these loose parameters, each offering its own pros and cons. In the end, we settled on an expanding polyurethane foam called Icynene. It's basically the same aerosol gap-sealing stuff that they sell in a can at the hardware store for filling in nooks and crannies around windows and doors—only on a much bigger scale. It doesn't burn quickly or rot, and it offers killer R-values. The obvious downside? Surprise, surprise—it would cost me a bundle. Spraying the Eco-Shed's walls and ceilings flush with expanding foam would set me back a whopping $5,215.20.

But the arguments for Icynene go on forever. The system is something of a darling in sustainable-building circles for its killer envelope-sealing qualities. The company is a member of the U.S. Green Building Council, the product is Energy Star–approved, and it's often featured in the American Lung Association's Health House program as an insulation that emits no gasses and keeps out dust, pollen, and other allergens. Even Tom Silva, the general contractor on public television's venerable *This Old House* loves the stuff; he has ordered it for more than one New England fixer-upper project.

Although Icynene's payoff horizon in a space as small as the Eco-Shed is basically never, there's still a lot to feel good about.

Given its void-filling properties and the way Parke designed the structure, the Eco-Shed will achieve theoretical insulation values of R-21.6 in the east and west walls, just shy of R-38 in the double north wall, and an impressive R-54 in the roof. Although actual performance levels will be slightly lower, this rating is way beyond what the code requires. And once installed, Icynene is inert, nontoxic, and nonallergenic. It will never sag or pinch or buckle and offers terrific soundproofing to boot. It's practically perfect. Sold!

Then the application crew showed up to install the product. And as the sprayer zipped himself into a Level 5 containment moon suit, complete with taped rubber gloves and a piped-in air supply, the reality of what I'd signed up for began to sink in. "You don't want to mess around with this stuff," the installer dude told me.

"Can I snap a few pictures of you in action?"

"You shouldn't be inside there at all without a mask on," Mr. Moon Suit replied.

Twenty minutes later, he was gunning my stud and rafter bays with foam that dramatically expands one hundred times its volume within seconds. I knew from seeing clips online that watching the stuff puff up is just the wildest thing, and I couldn't resist documenting the process. Against my installer's advice, I briefly ducked inside the Eco-Shed with my digicam.

Whoa, Nellie. The air inside my ecologically sensitive writing studio was so thick with toxic fumes that my chest immediately tightened, and after a minute my eyes began to water. The room had a heavy, unfamiliar, vaguely fruity chemical smell. After one or two snaps and a few seconds of video footage, I hastily beat a retreat. And it's a damn good thing I did, too.

Although Icynene is inert and nontoxic once reacted, or cured, in its pre-application, aerosolized form, it's not nearly so user-friendly. Only later, after considerable digging, did I learn that its primary ingredient is a compound called methylene diphe-nyl diisocyanate, or MDI, a substance from a family of industrial chemicals known as isocyanates. The company doesn't exactly advertise the fact, but according to the California Department of Health Services, isocyanates cause asthma and can also cause a lung disease known as hypersensitivity pneumonitis, the symptoms of which include fever, body aches, shortness of breath, and a cough with phlegm or sputum. The public agency notes that about one in twenty people who work with isocyanates may become sensitized to the chemicals; such people will suffer an asthma attack the moment they're exposed to even the smallest quantities of the stuff.

I had to ask myself if the American Lung Association was even in the same ZIP code while the moon-suited Icynene contractor went to work on its healthy-home project. And as I retreated from the poisonous haze swirling inside my so-called earth-friendly Eco-Shed, it occurred to me that perhaps rammed earth might have been the better route after all.

But every so-called green choice has its trade-offs. At some point along its life cycle, just about every substance we build with has some negative impact. The only solution is to do the homework and follow our gut instincts and moral compass. We could spend weeks investigating every aspect of a given building material—from its cradle to its gra ... er, cradle—and never find the right mix of compromises. My spray-foam insulation certainly unleashed its share of nasties during its manufacture and installation, but now that it is in place, it will theoretically help slash my energy use to a trickle over the lifetime of the building. As Cascadia Region Green Building Council CEO Jason McLennan likes to say, "Nothing is perfect in the material world except for straw, clay, and salvaged wood."

Well, I think to myself, at least I've scored one out of three.

⁂ *⁂* *⁂*

Once the eau du methylene diphenyl diisocyanate dissipated into the atmosphere, things started to move quickly. I tracked down a flavor of drywall with a high proportion of recycled gypsum content, and a boarding crew screwed it up on the walls and ceiling. My mudder and taper followed close behind, deftly repairing dings and hiding screw heads and seams. I polished the concrete floor and sealed it with a nontoxic water-based sealer. Cody Bentall's crew arrived to install the reclaimed cedar siding and flush the windows and door. It was time at last for the final accounting.

Over the past year and change—for about, gulp, ninety thousand dollars—I'd transformed the Eco-Shed from a slime-coated concrete sarcophagus into a soaring, cedar-trimmed studio worthy of a spread in a glamorous modern-design magazine. A few big to-dos remained to be checked off: The efficient electrical fixtures were back-ordered; ditto the bright modern tile, which, though manufactured by an environmentally responsible company, was en route to Bowen Island from—sorry, Gaia—Spain. But I'll be damned if the Eco-Shed wasn't just about finished.

Meanwhile, the ventilation system awaited Jeremy Galpin, who would theoretically return after his current off-island job was complete to build the utility cabinet, desk, and other millwork—but as far as my goals for energy efficiency were concerned, the studio was ready for its final exam. And the headmaster who would administer it was a man named Troy Glasner.

The owner of a start-up green-building consulting and services firm called E3 Eco Group, Glasner came over from the mainland one day in early October to perform a standardized evaluation and airtightness test on the Eco-Shed using a software package called Hot2000. When he's done, three hundred dollars later, he'll award me a score between 0 and 100. For me, the slavish approval-seeking perfectionist who has invested thousands of hours of sweat and toil into this project, a rating like this is pure crack cocaine. It's the objective score that I crave to validate everything I've done. In my mind, it is the project's defining hour, the part that really matters. Finally, I'll be able to transfer my work on the Eco-Shed into a bone fide approval rating.

To conduct his "blower-door" test, Glasner will first depressurize the Eco-Shed—he'll suck air out of the building with a large fan—and record where and how quickly the resulting vacuum pulls in replacement air through cracks and gaps in the walls and roof. He'll then feed his findings, plus a variety of other variables—such as my choices for insulation, heating, ventilation, glazing, foundation, and on-demand hot water—into Hot2000. Presto, just like that, his laptop will spit out my coveted Ener-Guide score.

Although an uninsulated building from the 1920s would likely rank in the teens, to score above an EnerGuide 90, I'd likely need to be in the realm of a superinsulated, off-grid, eco-palace clad in solar panels. In other words, the kind of pad only a retired rock star could afford. Since I was still working on my first hit single, I told myself I'd be happy with something in the mid-80s.

Glasner closed all the Eco-Shed's windows and sealed off all its various vents and ducts with sticky tape. As we chitchatted about the sorry state of the world, he opened the studio's front door wide and installed a nylon curtain called an infiltrometer in the opening, which he sealed tight against the top, bottom, and sides of the doorframe. Then he cinched a large electric fan into a fabric sleeve in the lower portion of the curtain and plugged in a pair of pressure gauges. One is labeled "room/house pressure"; the other "flow pressure."

After noting the studio's temperature (65.2 F) and humidity (62.4 percent), Glasner fired up the fan, which began evacuating air from the space. The gauge showing the pressure difference between the outside and inside of the building zoomed off the scale. We were in no danger of asphyxiating, but the space was much smaller than the 2,500-square-foot homes in which Glasner usually performs these audits, so he made some adjustments and hit the switch again.

Glasner recorded a few readings in his PDA, then it was time to play detective. "Wanna track down some leaks?"

I was bullish, of course. You would be, too, if you'd just dropped $5,215.20 to insulate a building the size of a one-car garage. This place was sealed up as if with Saran Wrap.

We walked around the room waving our hands at the walls and windows, trying to feel the rush of incoming air. And we didn't find much. "Wow, nice job," remarked my eco-auditor. "You've got nothing coming in around this window, nothing around the electrical boxes."

We did find some leaks here and there, though. I could detect a thin jet of air rushing in through a corner of the wall beside my large south-facing window. It's a spot where Galpin nailed together a vertical sandwich of three or four studs—a standard framing technique to accommodate two walls coming together at right angles to each other. The air was actually seeping in *between* the studs. Across the room, we found another hissing leak where a bundle of electrical cables emerged from the drywall inside a future cabinet. The Icynene crew entombed the wires in foam, but the sheetrock guys who followed inadvertently broke the airtight seal while wrestling them into place.

"You're in really good shape here," says Glasner. He went away for lunch for an hour and promised to return—having crunched some numbers on his laptop—with my EnerGuide score.

He came back scratching his head.

The verdict: "You're coming in at an 83," he said. "But, really, it should be higher than that."

That's barely an A, I think to myself.

"Huh. That's it?!"

"Yeah, that was my reaction, too," Glasner replied. "I suspect your studio is breaking my software. Because I should be able to change some of the variables and see that number move up and down, but I can't budge it."

"I'm not following you."

"Well, you have a really small space," he explained. "And everything about it is so bomber that I suspect the software is going, 'A space this small *can't* be this efficient, so I am going to stick you at a number and hold you to it.' And that number is 83."

As for air leakage, that value is harder to screw up, and I wished it were higher. If we rolled together all of the pinprick holes across the entire building envelope, the Eco-Shed has the equivalent overall leakage of a crack two inches wide by six inches long. Both scores are respectable—the average home clocks in at an EnerGuide 70, and any building above an 80 is considered highly efficient—but they're not the runaway full-scholarship smash hits I'd hoped for.

I was a little deflated. I thought about the time and money and sweat I'd invested in my green experiment; the risks I'd taken over the past year; the day care days spent planing down Peterson's siding; the neighborhood lobbying; the eleventh-hour concrete pours; the detective work and difficult trade-offs; and the financial pressures that still pressed down on me like a southbound flatcar stacked with certified lumber.

"You didn't fail any test here," Glasner offered. "I see a lot of buildings, and you've really done amazing work here. You've done everything right, you've set a new bar. And I've gotta tell you, there's something about your rating that does not compute."

Oh well, I reckoned, everything's relative. Perhaps we should run the blower-door test on the main house while Glasner was here with his gear. Then we'd get a sense of how much better I was doing with the sustainable-building strategies on display out here in the yard.

Glasner agreed. I'd already witnessed his infiltrometer drill, so I let him get on with it and returned to the sawhorses, where I was sealing the last of the Eco-Shed's reclaimed cedar siding.

A short while later, Glasner emerged from the house. And quite matter-of-factly, he told me that my nearly new, lightly greened spec home, under certain conditions, could kill me. Oh, and my family, too.

More specifically, my stylish, carbon-neutral, Danish wood-stove could do so—because if we have it going at the same time as all the kitchen and bathroom exhaust fans, the appliance will evidently dump odorless, colorless, and very deadly carbon mon-oxide into my home.

"What are you talking about?" I asked, incredulous.

"Well, I did your blower-door test—your house is pretty well sealed-up, by the way. And at the end of each test, I turn off the fan, let the air pressure equalize, and then turn on all the exhaust fans in the house. In your case, you've got your three bathroom fans and your range hood."

I recalled that we had specified an ultrapowerful kitchen exhaust to quickly evacuate cooking odors. "And?"

"Well, I turned on all the fans, and they started sucking air out of your house and pulling in replacement air through the cracks and fresh-air supply ducts in your house. Part of that sucking comes through my fan and registers on my pressure gauges. And when I did that, your house registered at seven pascals of pressure."

"And?"

"Anything above a five, in a combustion environment—which you have with your woodstove—that's where you get a danger. Because your fans are not getting the makeup air they need, and there is not enough of it coming into your house to supply the fire. And so what happens is the fans end up backdrafting air through your chimney and pulling carbon monoxide into your home with it."

I was gobsmacked. Out of the blue, almost by accident, Glasner had given me a little piece of beta that put all of my eco-hand wringing into perspective. While I've been fretting over cheap vinyl windows and making wise-ass cracks about the formaldehyde glue in my cabinets, a somewhat more pressing problem—technically, it's called combustion spillage—has been lurking in the shadows, waiting for an unusual, but not implausible, set of household conditions to converge, with potentially tragic consequences. It snapped everything into focus for me. It reminded me what is really important.

I do have a battery-powered carbon monoxide detector, so the future nightmare scenario that I would dream of in the weeks ahead was unlikely to unfold. But still. I resolved to correct the situation immediately.

"Thanks for stopping by and saving my life," I told Glasner as he packed up his truck. "I really appreciate that."

"Hey, don't even mention it."

12

The Epic Life

Each weekday at noon, the buzzer at Confederation Park Elementary School sounds for five long seconds like a klaxon scrambling a fighter wing. A roomful of seven-year-olds set down their Laurentian Pencil Crayons, grab their coats and lunchboxes, and file out the side door into the playground. The girls grab jump ropes and head for the basketball court, chasing and giggling. An alpha male picks up a checkered ball and heads the other way; the rest of the boys follow him, pushing and scrapping with each other. But one child hangs back, taking his own time in the cloakroom.

Standing on his toes, the lad carefully extracts a Great Grape Ape plastic lunchbox from his cubby, then trails his classmates out to the gravel parking lot, where a soccer game is already underway. He climbs onto one of the big granite boulders ringing the makeshift field, unwraps his peanut-butter-and-honey sandwich, and watches the other kids. And there he stays, sipping milk from a thermos and whiling away the hour in a state of profound boredom.

The playground monitors long ago gave up on encouraging the boy to join in. He has absolutely no interest in playing soccer, or, for that matter, any other group game of any kind, be it with ball, stick, hoop, or puck. In the "remarks" section of his mid-year report card, the lad's teacher, Mr. Calderone, will note his advanced reading skills—the towhead is digging into an account of the eruption at Pompeii—but also take care to flag the boy's unsettling antisocial behavior, carefully printing the six words that many Canadian parents would doubtless dread to read: "Jimmy does not like floor hockey."

More than three decades later—though this admission will doubtless shock and disturb many of my fellow countrymen—I still have only the vaguest understanding of hockey. Soccer is for me largely a mystery, and football remains one of the most cryptic and excruciatingly pointless exercises in Western civilization. I live in mortal fear of the day my son invites me down to the park to "toss the ol' pigskin around." It's not that I don't like sports per se, it's more that I've just never been much of a joiner.

All that said, I've been thinking about that bored boy on the granite rock quite a bit of late. Because somehow, remarkably, somewhere along the course of his freshman green year, the introverted tyke put down his Wonder Bread and jumped into the game. The construction project that began as a lark has evolved into what I can only describe as a calling.

My wife gave me a year and a generous slice of home equity to play with; in the end, she found herself with—yes, a second mortgage—but also a cute and sporty new car, a swish new studio, and what must at times feel like a whole new husband. In building my Eco-Shed, in lightening my transportation load, in engaging and connecting and, I hope, inspiring my friends and neighbors and relations—in deliberately shifting my head-space from obstacle to solution, from escapism to engagement, I'm feeling what I can only characterize as a sort of low-grade euphoria. It's a trickle of endorphin in my bloodstream, a feeling that I've signed on to something much bigger and more important than I am.

That's not to say that my green journey has purged me of my less-than-marketable character traits. My eco transformation isn't as tidy as a tear-jerker Hollywood ending: I'm still the kind of guy who chronically has one thing too many on the go, which is never a sustainable recipe. But if there is a lesson to be had from my first green year, it is simply that even the most jaded and dismissive son-of-a-bitch will find meaning, hope, and profound satisfaction when he starts taking charge of his destiny.

My old life ended for me the January night I successfully nudged the neighbors to conserve a little electricity. Having hardly so much as inked my name on a petition in the past, that evening kicked me further along a path I was already traveling. Instead of fretting over big, scary problems, I committed myself to fixing them. Even if it meant ruffling a few feathers now and again.

* * *

In the middle of September, I finally contacted my father-in-law to convey the difficult news about his carport. I didn't have the guts to call him, so I hit the keyboard. "This e-mail contains a few surprises," my confession began. "I hope you are sitting down."

Then I cut to the chase. "I have attached a photo showing our front yard as of a couple of days ago. The building is the green studio I have been working on since about March; I call it the Eco-Shed. You may have trouble getting your bearings with the picture because there is something missing: the carport. I am sorry to say that it does not exist anymore."

I then laid out the whole sordid saga, begged his understanding, and pressed Send. Elle and I waited for his reply. And waited. Hours became days, days became weeks. The balance of the month ticked away in uncomfortable silence. Even the dumb-blonde jokes stopped arriving in my e-mail box.

Finally, after twenty-one days without so much as a peep—without so much as a Photoshopped polar bear gag—we couldn't stand the suspense anymore. We'd not only expunged Padre's expensive carport from our property, but we'd also offloaded his luxury suv. Had my father-in-law disowned us in disgust? Elle picked up the phone and called him.

"Padre, it's me," my long-suffering wife said. "Do you hate us? Really? You *don't?!* Oh, we've been so worried!"

Pressing my ear to the back of the receiver, I could just make out the conversation.

"When were you guys planning on telling me?" Padre asked, laughing. He sounded a little wounded, but not critically. "The carport has been gone a long time, and you guys haven't even told me."

"We couldn't find the right way—we kept trying to find the right time and place and there just wasn't one. We've been wracked with worry about this for months. It was such a generous gift and we really tried to find a way to use it, but we couldn't make it work. You're not mad?"

"Of course not," Elle's dad said. "It's disappointing, and I guess I don't understand the decision. Don't you get something like a hundred and fifty days of rain a year up there? How are you going to unload the kids and the groceries in a downpour? Why would you rather have a studio that you don't really need than a carport protecting you?"

"Well, there's a big roof overhang on the studio," Elle offered, "so we can pull up next to that. But we are going to get wet, yes. I guess it doesn't bother us that much."

"Well, OK, but I'm a bit mystified. Say, 'Chelle, have you seen that new MacBook with a built-in video camera? I think I'm going to send you guys one, then we can make video phone calls on Skype. Won't that be a hoot?"

And that was more or less that. Things remain reasonably copacetic with Padre—he still thinks we made a bad call on the carport and at one point called the new and still-unfinished studio a "boondoggle"—but he still beams me the odd girlie picture and global-warming rant, so things can't be all that bad. I wish I could say the same thing about my relationship with his wife. Though I am certain time will heal all wounds, here in early 2008, our relationship remains a touch frostier. The point of friction with my step-mother-in-law is likely less the carport, and more the scorned vehicle we once sheltered within. It was she, you see, who used to drive the damn thing.

* * *

One soggy late-fall morning a couple of months later, I leaned halfway into the back seat of our new cherry-red Honda Fit to straighten out the kids' twisted seatbelts. Duncan wasn't making the task easy. Every time I thought I had the straps sorted out, Big Boy would reach over, giggle, and yank one of my ears. At which point I'd let go of the buckle, grab the little scamp by the chin, stare into his eyes, and remind him in a commanding tone that if he touched my ears one more time, I was going to wring his little ... er, I mean, I would have to confiscate his *Star Wars* comics indefinitely. Meanwhile, without any double carport sheltering me, I was getting drenched—just as Padre had promised.

I finally sorted everyone out, dashed back into the house to retrieve a forgotten lunchbox, collected my wits, stopped threatening my son, cranked the ignition, and put the car into reverse. The efficient little four-banger purred obediently as I backed out of the driveway and pointed us downhill towards the village. Along the way, the three of us silently took in the transportation profile of Bowen Island. Though there were a few other pint-size runabouts on the roads, we passed several contractors' Ram-tough megapickups, a jacked-up Ford Excursion with monster tires, and a bright-yellow Hummer H2. As we turned at the crossroads to motor up the hill towards the school, I waved hello—in the local style, with two fingers raised in a peace sign off the top of the steering wheel—at a few island yummy mummies I know, as they minivanned their way back home in the other direction.

We've seen all of these F-350s and Astrovans hundreds of times—in a small town, you know your neighbors by their wheels. But now, after a month or two spent cruising the island much closer to the ground, we've started to notice our new perspective on the world.

"Hey, Dad," asked Sabrina, "remember how you said our new car was much nicer to the planet?"

"Yeah?"

"That sounds pretty good to me."

"It does, doesn't it? I feel much better about our car. Don't you?"

"I guess so."

Then, a beat.

"But what about all the other cars?"

* * *

Yes, what about them? And for that matter, what about all the other houses, too, like the brand-new one next door—the one with more than a dozen exterior lights that cast useless ambience onto the surrounding hillside? And what about the rest of my neighbors, the ones I'd conscripted into my block-scale green movement almost a year ago with expertly roasted regional beef and local pinot noir? They were nowhere to be found. After a promising start, my optimistic plan to ignite neighborhood-scale grassroots change had fizzled. Gradually, over a period of months, with the exception of two diehard friends, pretty much everyone associated with the project drifted back to the business of their regular lives. Culdesactivism is a good idea—a clever catchphrase, certainly—but at this stage of our societal reinvention, it's perhaps not quite ready to catch fire.

Meanwhile, I was confronting a flame-out of another persuasion. The Eco-Shed had roughly another twenty thousand dollars' worth of work remaining to completion—millwork, heating, ventilation, tile, final plumbing and electrical, trim. I just didn't have it. The credit line was exhausted, the invoices past due. And one day, as I was rolling the second coat of low voc paint onto the studio's walls, my cell phone rang with a call to confirm it.

"Hi, James, it's Mike over at the credit union."

Mike was the branch manager, a young guy with nerdy glasses, in his late twenties. He'd recently become a dad for the first time. Mike had already upped my loan limit once. But something told me he wasn't calling me that day to set up a game of golf.

"Oh, hey, Mike. What's up?"

"Well, I'm just checking in because we've got an automatic funds transfer trying to pull money out of your account. It looks like it might be a life insurance premium?"

Bile began rising in my throat. Ah. The life insurance.

"Yeah, seems you don't quite have the funds in there to cover it. Do you want me to transfer in some money from your studio credit line?"

"Sure, go ahead and do that. I'm sort of juggling a little bit right now; I'm expecting some big paychecks that were supposed to have arrived by now."

Mike had gathered as much. He'd heard all about the Eco-Shed. He really liked what Elle and I were doing and supported us in our grand sustainability experiment. And why shouldn't he? There was no risk in it for him. If we couldn't come up with the green to pay for all the cutting-edge green I kept ranting on about, Mike's legal representative would one day come over and throw us—and all our possessions—out on the lawn. I wondered if Mike's next call might have a noticeably more businesslike tone.

But I wasn't going to let that happen. Spurred on by the notoriety and buzz generated from my new-model eco-home in miniature, all manner of interesting projects and contracts would doubtless begin heading my way. The kids would be done with expensive day care and preschool and finally into the school system. Meanwhile, I'd be raking in the bucks. Screw the occasional how-to magazine article at one dollar a word—there would be juicy consulting contracts, sky-high speaker's fees, lucrative retainers. I'd bill by the hour, net ten days, at ridiculous rates. The phone would barely stop ringing.

Eventually. Until then, I was just another debt-saddled client helping the credit-union manager meet his monthly minimum.

"I understand, James," said Mike. "Well, I'll go ahead and make that transfer. And in the meantime, let me know if there's anything I can do. Just keep me informed, OK?"

I knew at that moment that there would be no hemp-ribbon cutting ceremony starring Mayor Bob anytime soon; the Eco-Shed's completion would be a long, drawn-out, piecemeal affair. At least the building was sealed up for the winter. Whenever the clouds parted, it warmed up all by itself, as promised. But during the short days and long nights of windblown rain, I kept the building at a bare-minimum 55 degrees—and hopefully mold-free—with a small space heater connected to an outside receptacle via an extension cord. The umbilical was a temporary solution, but the fact remained: I was heating my Eco-Shed with the exact same kind of energy-sucking miniature toaster that did the honors inside my tract home—the cheapo, kilo-watt-hungry devices I'd allegedly sworn off once and for all.

In other words, I'd failed. I wasn't green; I was *almost* green. Although I had an efficient and impressive-looking—but not quite habitable—Eco-Shed in my yard, the grand adventure that I'd talked my overworked spouse into so many moons back felt on many days like a total flop. But I kept telling myself something (at least, when I had sufficient alcohol in my system): This story isn't yet finished.

* * *

"Congratulations, everyone," said Master Tony Kook, a fifth-degree black belt with the World Tae Kwon Do Federation and the owner of our island's training studio, or *dojang*. "You did really well tonight."

Here in the *dojang*, Elle and I—along with six of our fel-low students—had just passed our fourth Tae Kwon Do belt-promotion test. We're all lined up on the mat, standing tall in our sweat-soaked uniforms, feeling proud and strong.

Getting to this point had involved considerable effort, exhaustion, frustration, and sometimes risk and pain. Minutes before, Elle and I had each broken a three-quarter-inch-thick pine board with a carefully aimed knife-hand strike. But a fellow orange belt was not so successful. On his first try, he hesitated— or misjudged his force or aim—and the board refused to yield. Although the pain must have been intense, our pal's composure remained intact. Unfortunately, his hand did not: Days later, Elle saw him on the ferry sporting a cast. He passed the test on his second attempt, but the first impact fractured the fifth metacar-pal bone of his right hand.

After a year of twice-weekly training sessions, a half-dozen of us had kicked, punched, and blocked our way up through the junior levels of this Korean martial art—from white-belt begin-ner, to yellow-stripe, to yellow, and on up through orange. But, explained Kook, we were about to step out onto a whole new plateau.

"The theme of your new belt is patience," the master told us. "We have been moving through the early belts together quite quickly, but at this point, you are going to find your progress slowing down quite a bit," he explained. "You won't see the same rapid gains you have enjoyed up until now. Instead, we are going to have to take more time to perfect and build on the techniques we have learned so far. It is going to call for patience and per-severance, and you will see that through this patience comes growth."

Master Kook's remarks resonated with all of us, but especially with me—given the color of the stiff new cotton belt that I had just tied around my waist.

It was dark green.

* * *

Having stubbornly refused to compromise for the better part of a year, I now appreciate that green is more a direction than a destination. It is a relentless and private self-improvement project that will never be concluded. And this, I've realized, is precisely why I find it so appealing: it's an ever-receding horizon, an ever-levitating bar, and like the martial art of Tae Kwon Do, the greener life offers precisely that.

And as Elle, Duncan, Sabrina, and I zoom around the island in our shiny, smells-like-offgassing-plastic vehicle, pointing out Smart Cars—plus the odd Yaris or Penis, er, Prius—to our oil-addicted son along the way, we genuinely feel like we've lost a thousand pounds. There's room aplenty in here for all of us and all our stuff, too. And that may be the ultimate lesson of the carbon-reduced life that stretches before us. Yes, things are going to be different around here. And having had a taste of what it might look like, I bet you a six-pack of micro-brewed beer that it's going to change your world for the better, forever.

This is my chance to offer you a piece of advice, so here it is: Do something. Do it now. Dream up your own Eco-Shed, Eco-Car, Eco-Boat, Eco-Garden, Eco-Concrete, Eco-Whatever, and start on it today. Sit right up front and take charge of the process. Stop thinking about what you have to give up, or whom you might tick off, and start thinking about what you'll gain. Each of us must earn our own green belt at our own pace. But believe me, once you begin punching and kicking in that direction, you won't ever look back. And here's to that, friend, because your epic life isn't somewhere back there.

It starts here.

Acknowledgments

* * *

Almost Green would not have been possible without the support, encouragement, and input from a great number of individuals. Some of you helped me get to this point long before this book was even an outline; others offered crucial feedback on vague ideas and early drafts of the manuscript. Some of you simply watched my kids for a few hours here and there; others helped bring the Eco-Shed to life; still others provided various kinds of no-less-valuable contributions.

So props, then, to Bay Anapol, James Bannochie, Chris Barnett, Stacy Beamer, David Beers, Cody Bentall, Peter Boddy, Clemencia and Mike Braraten, Charles Campbell, Eliana Castillo, Stuart Cole, Douglas Coupland, Peter Dean, Tony Dominelli, Peter Duplessis, Hal Espen, Jane Ferguson, Oscar Flechas, Nancy Flight, Helen Goodland, Ruth Harding, Keyolynn Hayward, Nick Heil, Tony Hilliard, David Hocking, Burns Jennings, Corbin Keep, Morganne Keplar, Martha Magor,

Vanessa Matthews, Anne McDermid, Charles Montgomery, Michael Mullen and North Shore Credit Union, Julie, Brad, Kathryn, and Adam Ovenell-Carter, Padre and Cher, Dan Parke, Jean-Paul Poirier, Gary Ross, Tobyn Ross, Rob Sanders, Arno Schmidt, Greg Shea, Karyln and Gordon Shepherd, Greg Sims, Scott Sinclair, Brando Skyhorse, Dave Stalker, Jim Sutherland, Tom Taylor, and Bob Turner.

Special thanks to Mum and Dad for believing in me and jumping in to help when the chips were down. I love you both.

Finally, you would not be holding this book in your hands were it not for my dear wife, Elle, an endlessly renewable source of love, spirit, and support. Thank you for indulging me, subsidizing our almost-green life, and believing in me more than I usually believe in myself.